Anti-Environments

On the Exploration of Unconventional Tools through Friction and Norm-Bending

Produced in Google Sheets

“For all the things I interact with and never noticed.”

Borchardt, L. (2025)

Introduction

Digital design today is characterized by seamless processes. Software tools work smoothly, workflows promise efficiency, interfaces are—or appear to be—self-explanatory. But it is precisely this seamlessness that poses a risk. If every form of irritation is eliminated, differentiation, spontaneity, and critical distance begin to vanish. When design unconsciously submits to standards or tools, it loses variety and depth.

That is what this book, Anti-Environments, takes as its starting point. It explores how unconventional perspectives on digital tools and alternative design processes can unlock new creative potential. Potential that goes beyond pure functionality and leads to increased autonomy and experimental practices when working with digital media. At its core is engagement with

friction: points of resistance, irritations, and limitations that are understood not as disruptions, but as productive conditions for design. Where tools do not provide automated solutions, friction arises, forcing reflection and opening up spaces beyond familiar paths.

This collection brings together tools that challenge the conventions of software interaction in different ways. Among them are creative-coding programs that isolate specific aesthetic possibilities and enable them to be investigated; software originally developed for entirely different purposes but which, through subversion, offers new forms of expression; and interfaces that prompt alternative modes of interaction. Such tools demonstrate that digital media do not merely depict linear processes, but can be seen as dynamic, form-giving systems, as media that can be used, questioned, and repurposed. Anti-Environments itself is a product of this same logic. Designed and created entirely in a spreadsheet application, Google Sheets, the book incorporates the very conceptual framework and content it describes. When a seemingly unsuitable tool becomes a medium, a practice of subversion—or repurposing—emerges that generates friction and reveals new perspectives. One advantage of this hybrid publishing concept is that it allows readers to print and bind the book themselves. In this openness lies a democratic impulse: knowledge is made accessible and design is released from the closed economies of proprietary software environments. The outcomes of these exploratory encounters are documented in

images that make visible the processes and results of working with unconventional tools. Many of these works are accompanied by quotations that reflect on digital technologies and the potential of friction, creating a loose narrative structure throughout the book. In addition, selected tools that have proved to hold particular potential are contextualized through short introductory reflections.

Anti-Environments is more than a collection of experimental tools. It urges us not just to see tools as something to be used, but also to question, reinterpret or even design them ourselves, implementing them as media for aesthetic research. It advocates for a practice that does not circumvent resistance, but renders it productive, against the seamlessness of standardized workflows, in favor of the diversity of the unpredictable.

Anti-Environments: On Tools, Friction, and Aesthetic Inquiry

Marshall McLuhan coined the term "anti-environment" to describe a concept that at first glance seems paradoxical. While environments usually operate unnoticed in the background, subtly shaping our perception, an anti-environment constitutes a counter-situation that breaks through this invisibility. Anti-environments provide contrast. They disrupt the familiar and thereby render it visible.

They create distance from habitual patterns and enable us to perceive and reflect on conditions more consciously. Design practice is profoundly bound to tools. They not only determine the means available to us but also shape how we think, perceive, and make decisions. Tools are usually regarded as neutral instruments that merely support the creative process. But actually they provide a framework. They structure processes, suggest modes of use, and influence aesthetic outcomes.

Tools as Invisible Infrastructures

Marshall McLuhan coined the term "anti-environment" to describe a concept that at first glance seems paradoxical. While environments usually operate unnoticed in the background, subtly shaping our perception, an anti-environment constitutes a counter-situation that breaks through this invisibility. Anti-environments provide contrast. They disrupt the familiar and thereby render it visible. They create distance from habitual patterns and enable us to perceive and reflect on conditions more consciously. Design practice is profoundly bound to tools. They not only determine the means available to us but also shape how we think, perceive, and make decisions. Tools are usually regarded as neutral instruments that merely support the creative process. But actually they provide a framework. They structure processes, suggest modes of use, and influence aesthetic outcomes. McLuhan captured this insight back in the 1960s with his famous statement, "the medium is the message" (McLuhan 2003: 7). Media and tools are not passive carriers of content; they actively shape the message itself by directing perception and communication. In this sense, it is not only the content that matters but also the form into which it is rendered by the medium.

This interrelation becomes particularly obscured in the realm of digital design tools. Software creates the impression of being a universal, open instrument offering neutral freedoms. Yet every interface contains implicit assumptions about which methods are intended, which aesthetics are deemed desirable, and which actions appear efficient. Presets, menus, icons, and workflows form an invisible framework that channels the design process along specific paths.

Crucially, this framing is not generally perceived or reflected upon. Digital tools appear self-evident, almost invisible. Or, as McLuhan provocatively put it, "If it works, it's obsolete" (McLuhan 2010: 139). Technologies vanish from our awareness as soon as they function seamlessly. The less friction an interaction entails, the less we notice the structures that guide our actions. It is precisely in this invisibility that their power resides. The ubiquitous tools we use every day are not merely a means

of execution. They are also decisive factors in shaping the standards and norms that define design practice. They determine how we define efficiency, professionalism, or originality This raises a fundamental question. What possibilities emerge if these seemingly neutral frameworks are not simply accepted but consciously interrogated and disrupted?

The Comfort of Standards

The invisibility of digital tools becomes particularly evident in their standardization. Already in the first semesters of design degrees, students are introduced to the Adobe Creative Suite as the essential foundation, often accompanied by a recommendation to work on Apple hardware. This combination of software and operating system is widely regarded as a prerequisite for professional design, taken for granted much like pen and paper. The choice of tools is not presented as an option but as a normative requirement.

This monopoly extends into the professional sphere. Adobe software dominates, accounting for around 80 percent of the global creative market. Even free alternatives such as Gimp, Inkscape, or Krita align themselves closely with Adobe's functional logic in order to ensure compatibility The industry standard thus becomes a global foundation that permeates both education and practice. What may appear to be a shared basis in fact leads to a homogenization of workflows. German designer Markus Weisbeck observes this development with a critical eye: "Today, designers across the globe are all using very similar tools and methods. And there is a tendency towards a somewhat synchronized style being paraded by design blogs, which also produces a certain unification of modern world taste." (Weisbeck & Palko 2017: 9). The worldwide availability of identical software packages, combined with the algorithmic visibility of similar design solutions across digital media, has created a synchronized style that flattens diversity rather than fostering it.

Standardized tools provide efficiency, predictability, and economically attractive modes of production. Yet they also establish a comfort zone in which deviations are increasingly marginalized. Routines and predefined workflows relieve designers of complex decisions, while the focus shifts: instead of actively questioning tools, attention is directed toward their smoothest possible application. Tools become blind spots, structuring the framework without themselves becoming subjects of critical reflection.

This creates a paradoxical relationship: the more software facilitates creative processes, the more creative autonomy is lost. The comfort of standardization accelerates workflows but simultaneously reduces the friction necessary to unlock new design possibilities. Design adapts itself to the structures of its tools, rather than having those tools adapt to design.

The Paradigm of Technological Invisibility

The standardization of common tools leads to a homogenization of aesthetic outcomes while reinforcing the invisibility of digital technologies. The more smoothly software functions, the less it is perceived as an active agent in shaping design. This invisibility is not accidental but the result of a central paradigm in software development: user-centered design. Its core aim is to make interactions as intuitive, efficient, and error-free as possible. Potential points of resistance must be minimized, difficulties eliminated, complexities concealed. Interfaces give the impression that technology adapts to our needs, while in reality it is structuring our actions through predefined patterns and routines. This produces a paradox: the simpler systems appear to us, the more complex they are internally. Digital technologies evolve at high speed, their technical infrastructure becoming increasingly inaccessible. For users, this creates a distance that obstructs deeper engagement. Today, interaction has been reduced to a handful of standardized gestures, such as typing, swiping, and clicking, while systems' underlying logic remains hidden. The result is a sense of self-evidence that easily slips into passivity. Digital technologies seem like a kind of magic, reliably fulfilling their function without requiring us to understand how they do so. We move along smoothly paved paths, their direction predetermined by developers, and increasingly by AI. But if we leave these paths, we are confronted by a thicket of inaccessibility and technical complexity that seems nearly impenetrable. When tools become invisible, we enter a relation of dependency. We accept their prescriptions without reflection and subordinate our work to the structures of software. The technology does not truly disappear. It merely vanishes from sight, while its internal complexity further obstructs our access.

Friction as a Gateway to Innovation

In everyday understanding, friction is usually regarded as an obstacle. It stands for resistance, delay, disruption, for everything that slows down or complicates processes. Yet in creative and design practices, friction develops a distinctive quality. It compels us to engage, interrupts routines, and thereby opens new perspectives. In The Reflective Practitioner (1983), Donald Schön states that unexpected difficulties are an essential part of professional practice. Designers encounter

problems that cannot be solved through routine knowledge but demand reflection. These "frictive moments" foster critical thinking and lead to more sustainable solutions. Similarly, John Maeda formulates his concept of "creative tension" in The Laws of Simplicity (Maeda 2006), stating that innovation arises not despite but precisely through contradictions and conflicts. Herbert Simon had already emphasized in The Sciences of the Artificial (Simon 1969) that design processes are always a balancing act between possibilities and constraints, and that it is within this tension that the true power of design lies.

Friction means that habitual processes come to a halt. These interruptions redirect attention toward the medium itself: not solely toward content, but toward the structures that produce it. Only in the moment of irritation does the tool become visible, as an active factor that influences our actions.

Artistic practice offers numerous examples of how productive friction can be. John Cage, for instance, composed his Suite for Toy Piano (composed 1948; Johncage.org 2023) for a children's piano whose limited tonal range and sonic weaknesses made the faithful realization of a classical piece impossible. Yet it was precisely these inadequacies that generated a new aesthetic beyond the expected. Designer Martin Venezky similarly pursues strategies of deliberate difficulty. In keeping with a "design made difficult" approach, he employs unsuitable tools or cumbersome methods in order to disrupt routines and provoke unforeseen outcomes (Weisbeck & Palko 2017).

In her manifesto, Designing Friction (Maurer & Wouters 2023), designer Luna Maurer emphasizes the necessity of deliberately seeking friction in digital practice. She names four approaches: first, actively pursuing discomfort by leaving familiar comfort zones; second, introducing deliberate delays in time to counter the obsession with speed and instant gratification; third, breaking through standardized interfaces to re-involve the body with interactions; and fourth, accepting imperfection, which digital processes often systematically eliminate. These strategies demonstrate that friction is not merely a disturbance but a driving force behind creative processes. It interrupts what is taken for granted, draws attention to structures, and makes room for discovery. A design process that proceeds entirely without friction may yield efficiency but remains superficial. Only where ruptures, obstacles, and resistance arise does it become possible to develop new ways of thinking and acting. In a time defined by speed, perfection, and optimization, friction therefore acquires particular significance. It stands as a counter-principle to seamless functioning, a moment of pause, irritation, and reflection. For design, this means that friction is not to be avoided but deliberately cultivated. It is a condition for innovation, critical thought, and aesthetic diversity.

Subversion as a Creative Strategy

A particular strategy, independent of pure friction, is subversion. This means using existing tools in ways that run counter to their intended function, probing their limits, and uncovering new modes of expression. This practice reveals with particular clarity that tools are not neutral instruments but negotiation spaces that can be transformed by creative appropriation. A striking example comes from the Indigenous artist Sharol Graves. In the mid-1980s, while working in Silicon Valley, she used CAD/CAM software to create Indigenous patterns during her lunch breaks. This was neither intended nor supported by the tool, which was actually designed to develop electronic circuits. The system crashed regularly and the plotter refused to output Graves' images, but she found ways to outwit it. "I made the computer do things the software wasn't designed to do," she later explained (Graves 1995: 9). Her practice was not only a technical act but also a cultural one. She infiltrated a system that actually excluded her and revealed that alternative spaces of expression exist beyond the hegemonic narratives of Silicon Valley.

Subversion, then, is not merely resistance but also a form of inquiry. Digital tools harbor far more potential than their manuals or interface designs suggest. The widespread practice of using a specialized program for every specific task—Photoshop for photographs, InDesign for layouts, Premiere for film—reduces tools to linear, predetermined pathways. The contemporary app economy has intensified this fragmentation. Yet it is precisely "incorrect" or unconventional use that opens up new perspectives. Photographs can be manipulated in audio software such as Audacity; books can, as this very project demonstrates, be designed in Google Sheets. Such approaches reveal that digital artifacts are not one-dimensional. They can be understood as multi-layered reservoirs of design and aesthetic possibility. For designers, this implies understanding themselves as researchers of aesthetic potential. Their task is not limited to producing (functional) outcomes. It includes investigating existing systems for hidden forms of expression. Subversion broadens the field of design, demonstrating that tools are not fixed but can be reinterpreted through creative practice. At the same time, this stance carries a political dimension. In a world where a handful of corporations dictate the standards of digital tools, subversion becomes a way of resisting their normative power. It opens up spaces beyond predictable workflows and enables autonomy within structured dependencies. When designers subvert tools actively rather than simply adopting them passively, they engage in a practice that both exposes power relations and generates new aesthetic forms. Therefore, subversion is not only

a design method but also an attitude. It reflects a willingness to leave behind the comfort of standards, to accept the fragility of digital systems, and to discover new possibilities in resisting routines. The crucial element of this attitude is to refuse to accept digital tools as predetermined frameworks and instead to approach them as open fields of creative and cultural engagement.

From Users to Toolmakers

Engagement with tools is not limited to using them. The boundaries between users and developers are becoming increasingly blurred, with designers themselves becoming toolmakers. This transition opens new scope for action, as the technical layer is no longer accepted merely as a given condition but is actively altered, expanded, and shaped. This becomes especially evident in the field of creative coding. Here, programming languages are not used solely for utilitarian development but are understood as creative instruments. Designers write their own scripts, devise experimental interfaces, or generate visual systems that diverge markedly from established software paradigms. This practice combines reflection and production, with the tools themselves becoming artifacts whose form and function are continuously being negotiated. The open-source culture reinforces this process. It not only enables access to existing systems but also their modification and further development. Instead of understanding tools exclusively as closed products from large corporations, collaborative ecosystems emerge in which designers can adapt, exchange, or recombine functionalities. In this way, design becomes not only a matter of content but also, infrastructurally, a field of aesthetic and political engagement. This approach is particularly relevant for communication design. Unlike many other professions, it enables you to combine analysis and practice. Designers are not bound exclusively to efficiency or correct tool use; they also have the freedom to question conventions and develop alternative practices. Universities play a key role here, as they offer spaces where experimenting with tools can be encouraged and critically reflected on, away from professional routines.

Students in particular have the opportunity, and perhaps the responsibility, to transform tools actively as well as simply using them. By questioning, adapting, or even creating tools themselves, they gain deeper awareness of the structures shaping their work. This is the precise interface where anti-environments emerge: when tools are no longer treated as self-evident instruments, but become the subject of design reflection and production. Designers thus increasingly inhabit a dual role: as producers of visual outcomes and as developers of the systems that enable these outcomes. By combining both roles, they not only expand their own scope of action but also create new forms of autonomy in a field otherwise strongly shaped by standardization.

Anti-Environments as a Design Approach

Anti-environments are not just a theoretical concept, but also constitute an approach within design practice. They emerge where tools do not function seamlessly but instead cause irritation, where they generate friction rather than being absorbed into routines. This friction provides an opportunity to realign perception. Tools are no longer taken for granted, but become visible as formative factors that shape how we think and act. This book itself is an anti-environment. It was a deliberate decision not to use classical layout programs such as InDesign. Instead, the book was created entirely in Google Sheets, software that was developed for tabular data processing and is by no means intended for book design. This repurposing results in multiple moments of friction: workarounds, restrictions, technical limitations. But it is precisely these confrontations that render the act of designing visible. Each step becomes a reflection on the possibilities and limitations of the tool. This both reveals a design experiment and articulates a stance. Anti-environments counter the passivity that arises from standardized, frictionless processes. They urge us to question routines, test alternatives, and regain autonomy when engaging with digital media. This stance includes resistance against the homogenization of aesthetic outcomes as well as a call for the unpredictable, the unfinished, and the experimental.

Anti-Environments should be read as a collection of unconventional tools, and also a call for a more deliberate design practice. The point is not simply to apply new tools but to renegotiate the relationship between humans and tools. By allowing, seeking, and enduring friction, by practicing subversion, and by developing our own tools, we expand the horizons of aesthetic and cultural design. Anti-environments stand for a practice that does not simply employ digital tools but understands them as open, negotiable media, spaces where new perspectives can emerge.

McLuhan, M. (2003):
Understanding Media:
The Extensions of Man. Corte Madera,
CA: Gingko Press.

McLuhan, M. (2010):
The Medium and the Light:
Reflections on Religion and Media. Eugene,
OR: Wipf and Stock Publishers.

Weisbeck, M. & Palko, A. (2017):
Space for Visual Research 2:
Workshop, Manual and Compendium.
Leipzig: Spector Books.

Schön, D. A. (1983):
The Reflective Practitioner:
How Professionals Think in Action.
New York: Basic Books.

Maeda, J. (2006):
The Laws of Simplicity:
Design, Technology, Business, Life.
Cambridge, MA: MIT Press.

Simon, H. A. (1969):
The Sciences of the Artificial.
Cambridge, MA: MIT Press.

Johncage.org (2023):
Suite for Toy Piano, John Cage Complete Works.
Available at: https://www.johncage.org/pp/John-Cage-Work-Detail.cfm?work_ID=196
(last viewed: 3.9.2025).

Maurer, L. & Wouters, R. (2023):
Designing Friction.
Available at: https://designingfriction.com/
(last viewed: 3.9.2025).

Graves, S. (1995):
"Indian Circuits".
In: Bates, S. (ed.): Indian Humor.
San Francisco: American Indian Contemporary Arts.

Mono Tool

This is an interactive tool by Lena Weber that enables you to create abstract shapes and gradients. Its interface is based on a grid that allows you to experiment with stylistic elements and use random gradients to generate shapes and compositions. Within the grid, elements can seamlessly merge, overlap, and stretch.
By introducing deliberate constraints, the tool encourages users to adopt a new way of working and intentionally omits the option to undo individual steps. Accepting “mistakes” and unforeseen outcomes plays a central role, often enriching the creative process and challenging perfectionist design approaches.

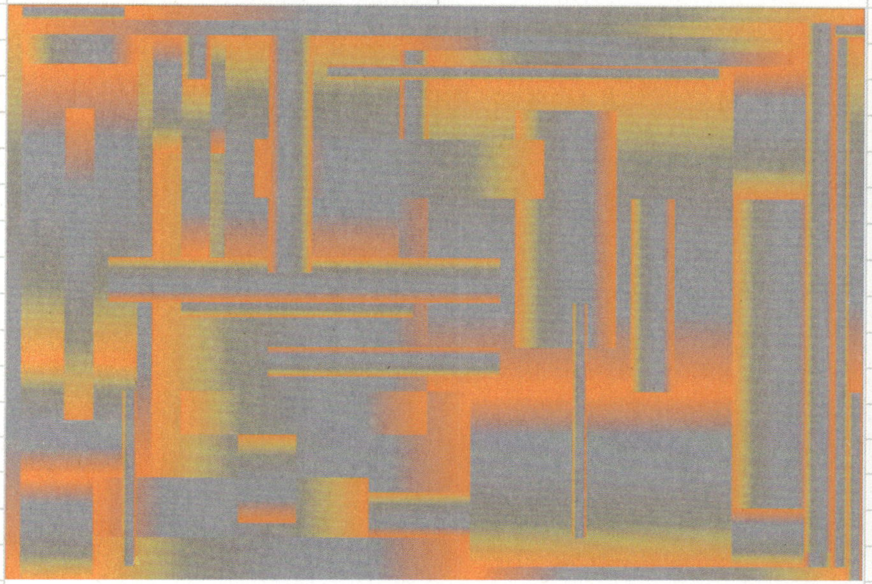

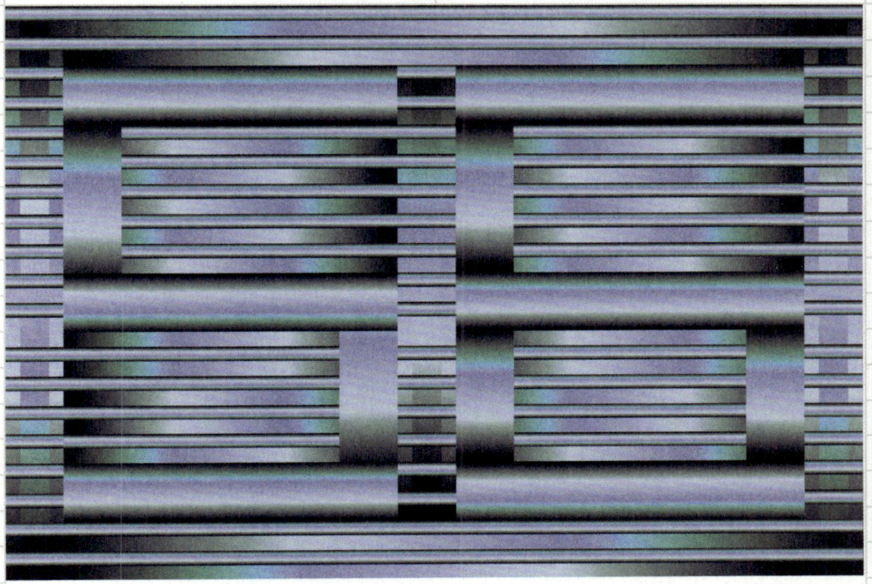

Anti-Environments

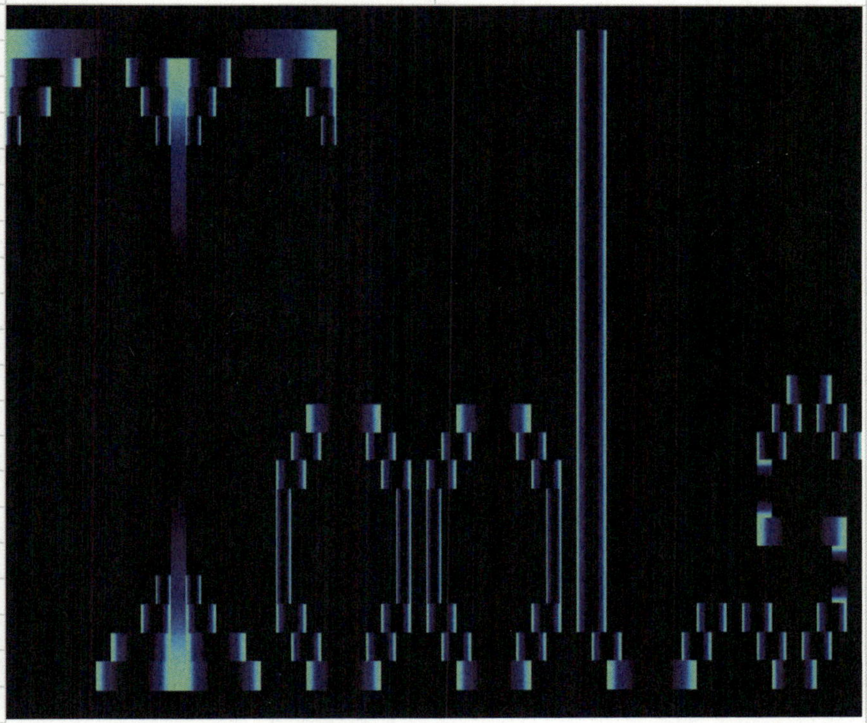

Mono Tool

Plotter Tool

Plotter by Florian Gubernator is a tool based on the p5.js library that simulates a digital pen writing a previously entered sentence onto a canvas. While the pen draws the letters in precise movements, the user can move the canvas itself. This interaction shifts the position where the pen writes, resulting in distortions and unusual shapes. You can also adjust parameters such as pen size, speed, and color. New canvases can be created, layered, and later exported as individual images. If you want to correct something, the only options are to lift the pen or reset the entire process.

Unlike in conventional graphic design programs, where the canvas remains a static element, in Plotter it becomes an active control element in itself. This shift in perspective makes the process both unfamiliar and challenging. An otherwise passive element moves into the foreground and has a direct influence on the design. The associated loss of control opens up the possibility of producing results beyond digital perfection, works that oscillate between precise rigor and analog irregularity, giving rise to a hybrid aesthetic. Particularly noteworthy is how the tool productively blurs the boundary between designing and controlling.

Our tools are now often so flawlessly smooth that we stop noticing —let alone questioning— them.

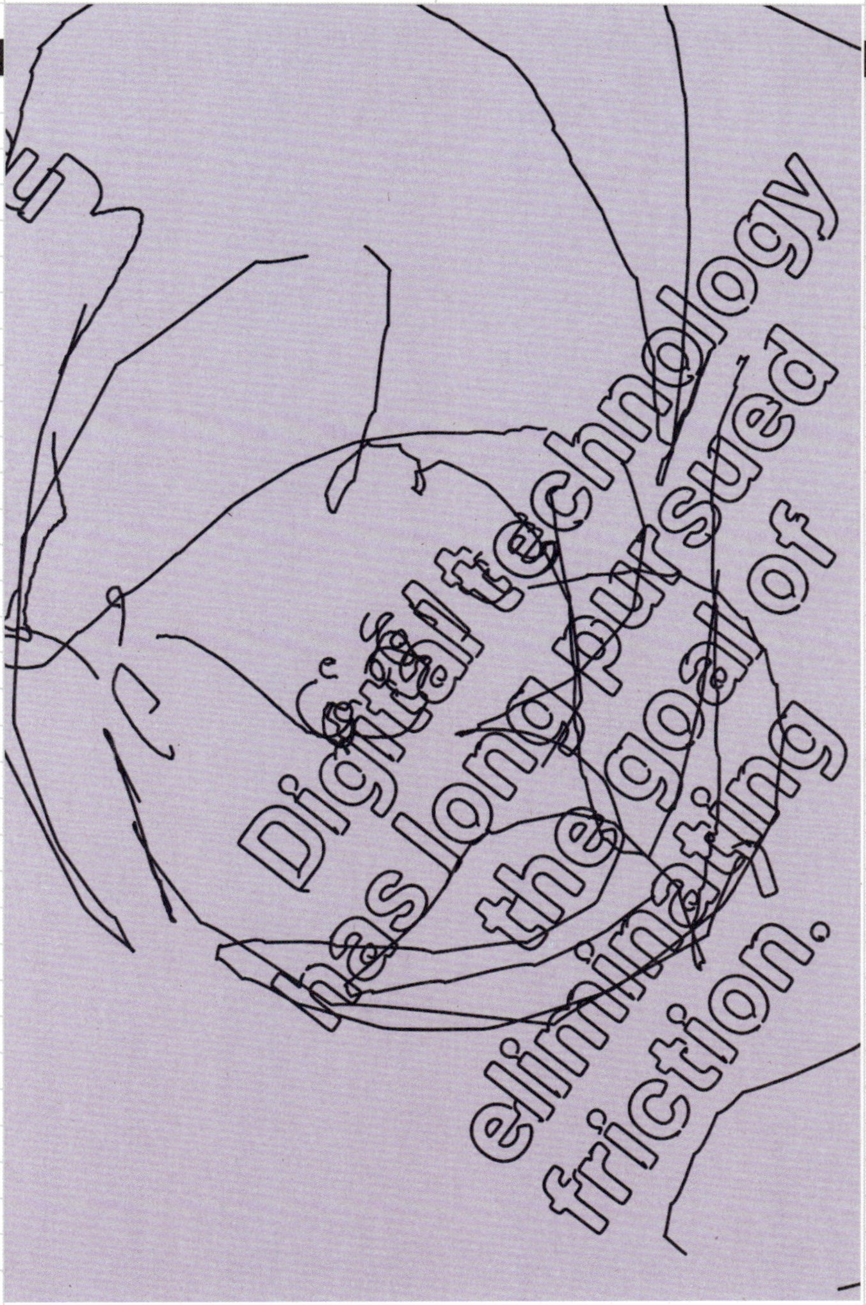
Digital technology
has long pursued
the goal of
eliminating
friction.

We have strived to
design 'seamless'
digital systems in
which users go about
completing their
goals with little awareness of
underlying technology,
where things happen
'automagically'.

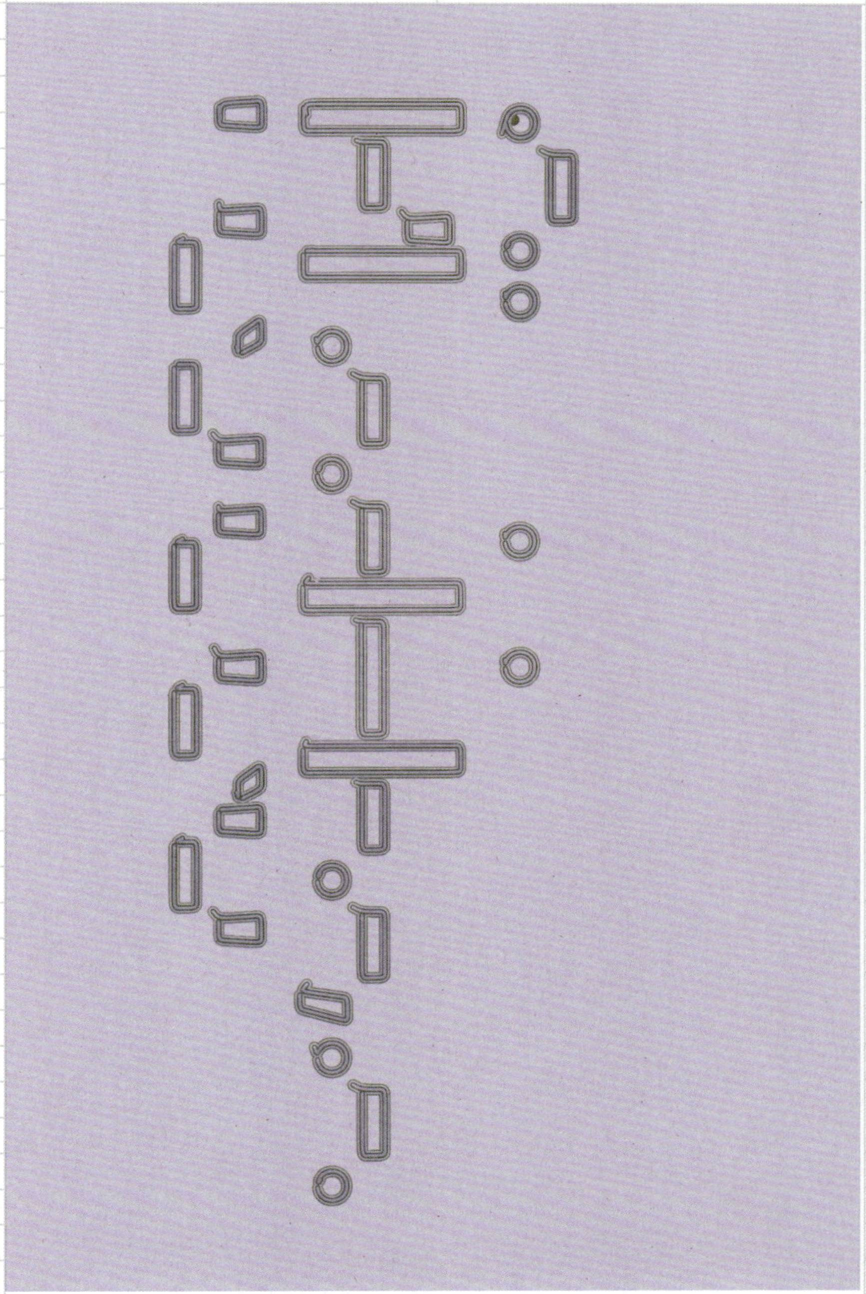

Hold down [shift] to move the paper without rotating

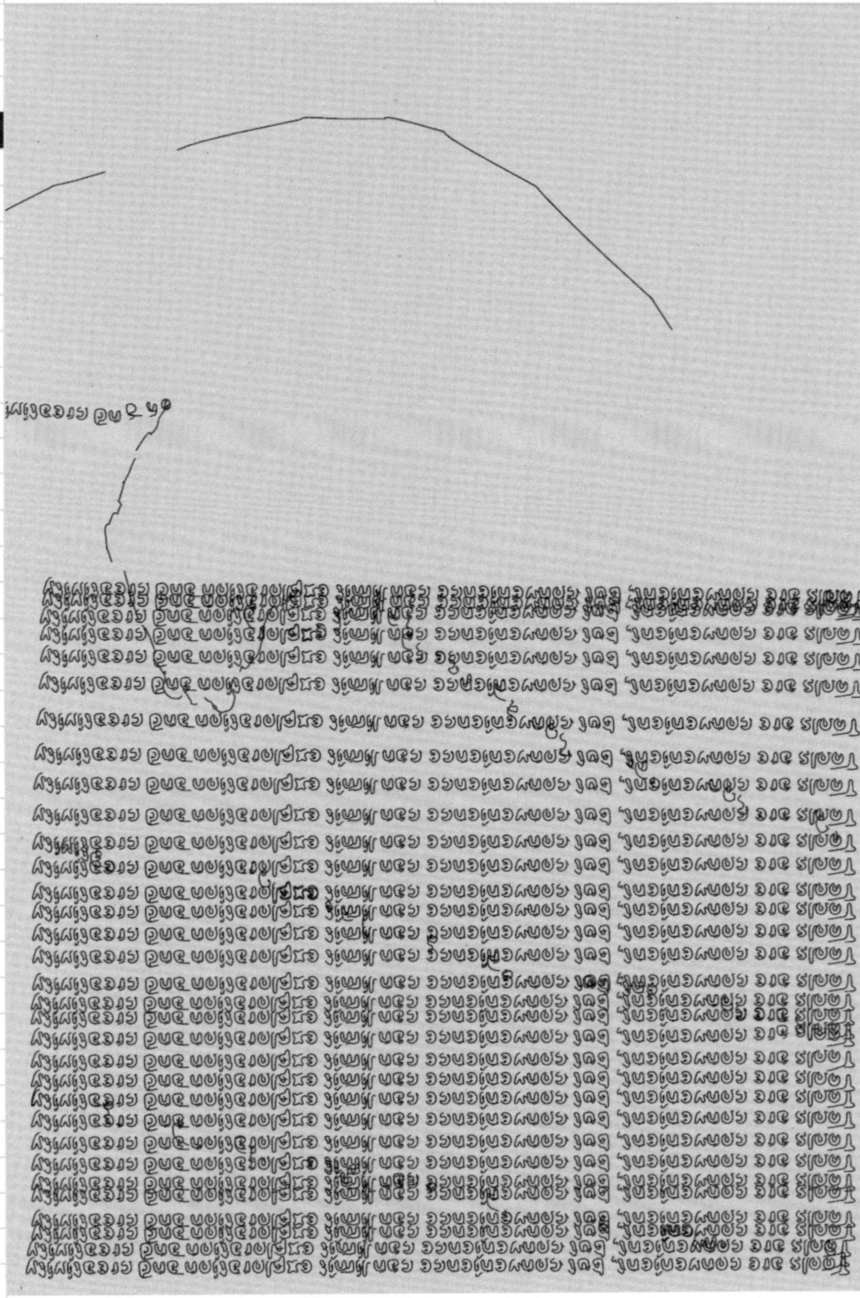

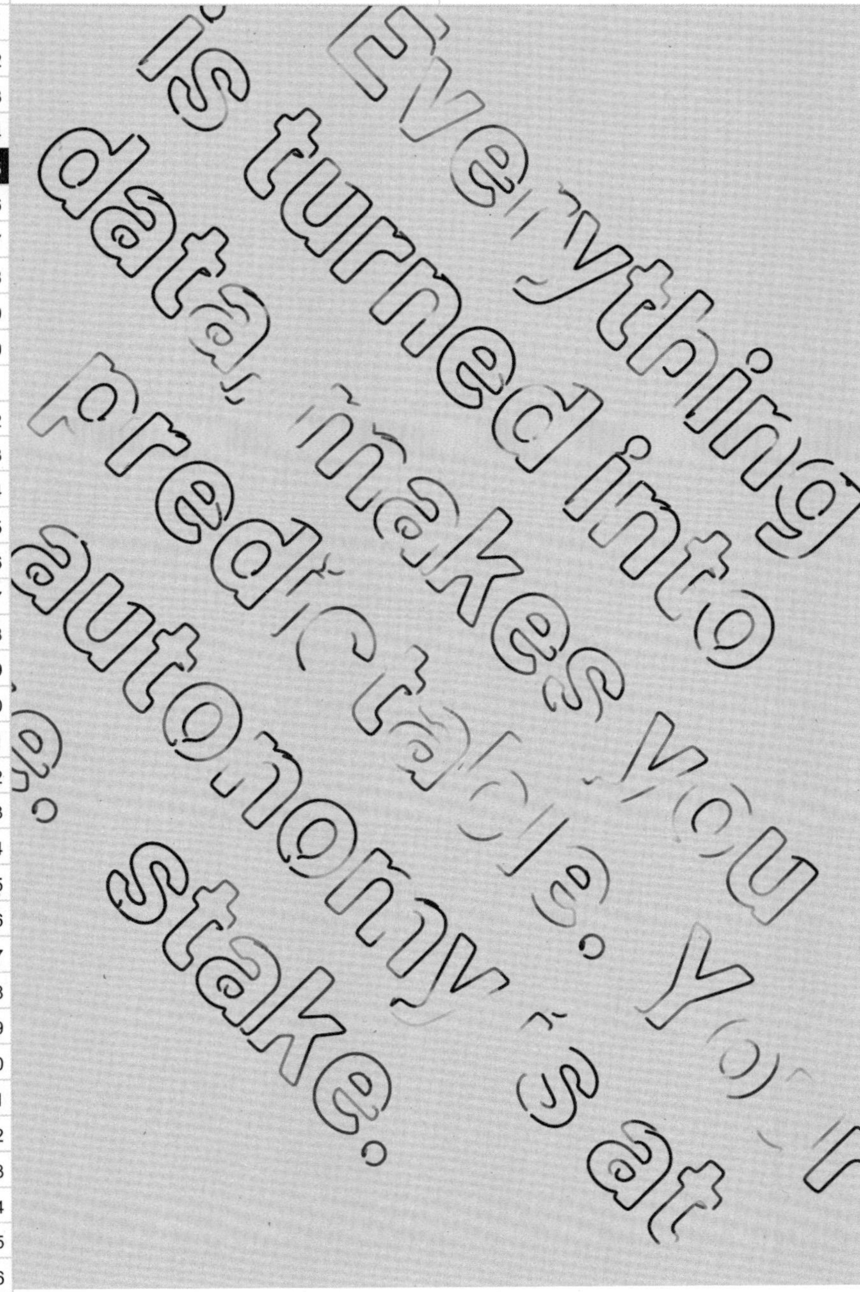
Everything
is turned into
data, makes you
predictable. Your
autonomy is at
stake.

So, if we are
predictable,
if our environment
is predictable, a
few people
can control it
better

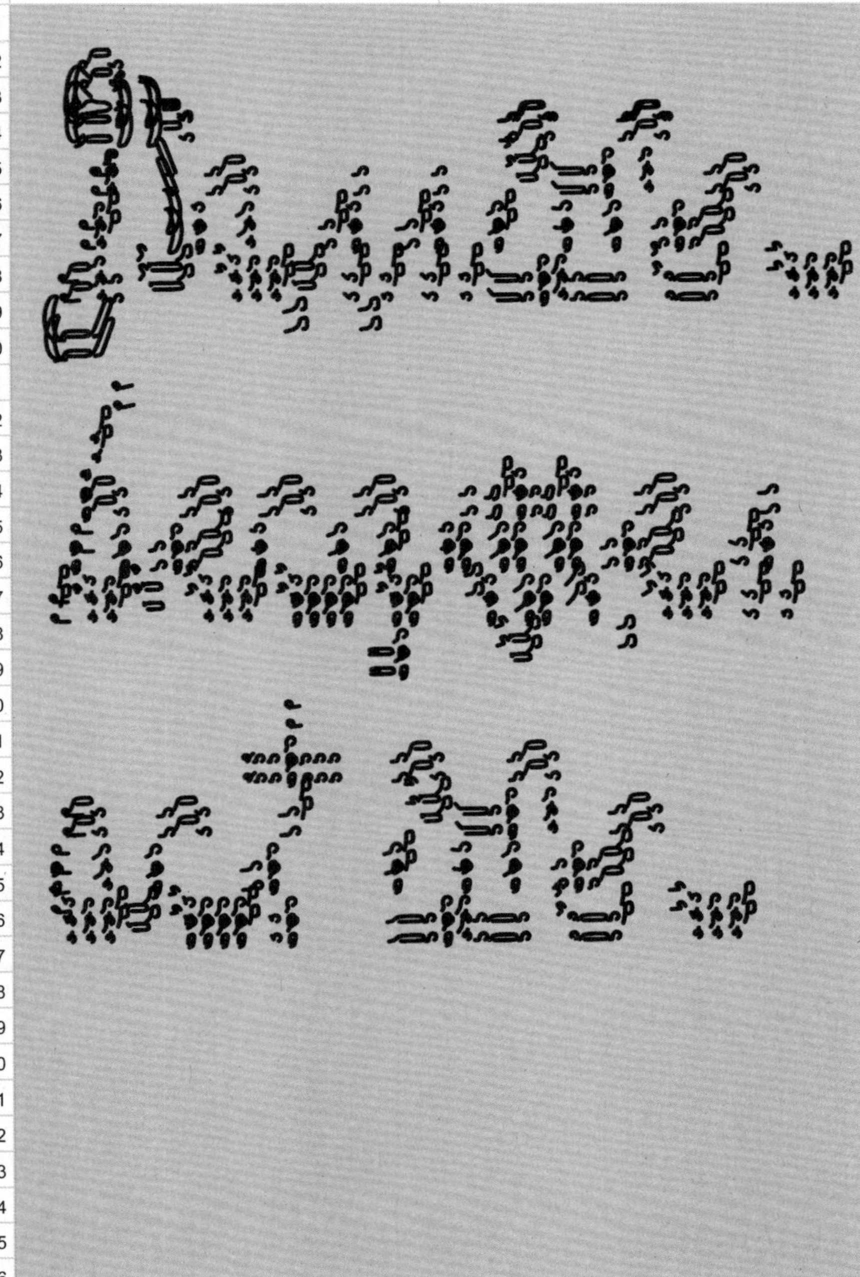

As designers
we have been
relentless about
prioritizing
ease-of-use, identifying
friction and
eradicating
it from the interactions
we design.

super

Audacity

Audacity is a free, cross-platform, open-source program for editing and recording audio. It features a functional interface with a timeline, toolbars, and audio tracks. Users can import, cut, copy, and mix audio files, as well as applying effects such as noise reduction, equalization, or pitch and speed adjustment. Audacity supports a wide range of audio formats and allows multi-track recording, spectrogram analysis, and precise editing through zoom and marker functions. The program also offers plugin support, enabling extended functionality through effects and analysis tools. Audacity was first released in 2000 by Dominic Mazzoni and Roger Dannenberg at Carnegie Mellon University and has since become one of the most widely used open-source audio editors.

Although Audacity was originally developed as a music-editing program, it can also be repurposed for image manipulation using so-called data-bending. Image files are first converted into a format that supports audio (such as Bitmap), then opened in Audacity and processed with effects. Interventions such as equalizers, distortions, or the shifting of data blocks produce visual disruptions and abstract glitches once the file is reconverted into an image format.

The editing is done using auditory tools, while the image itself remains invisible. So the user works “blind” until the image is converted back in the final step. This shifts the process. Instead of users having precise control over editing, the focus moves toward an exploratory engagement with data structures, their resilience,

and the interplay between auditory effects and visual outcomes. Differences between formats become particularly evident. While PNG files “break” after even minimal interference, JPGs require more radical manipulation before visible changes appear. Some formats, such as WEBP, yield characteristic wave-like distortions, while others display more unpredictable transformations.

With sustained exploration, Audacity ceases to be understood as a mere audio program. Those who systematically examine the effects can develop targeted operations and combinations that at times resemble filters from conventional image editing software. Repurposing Audacity shifts the focus from the visible surface to the material foundations of digital images: coding, data blocks, and error

resistance. Here, design is not mediated solely through visual interfaces, but through technical structures, an approach that is at once experimental, investigative, and speculative.

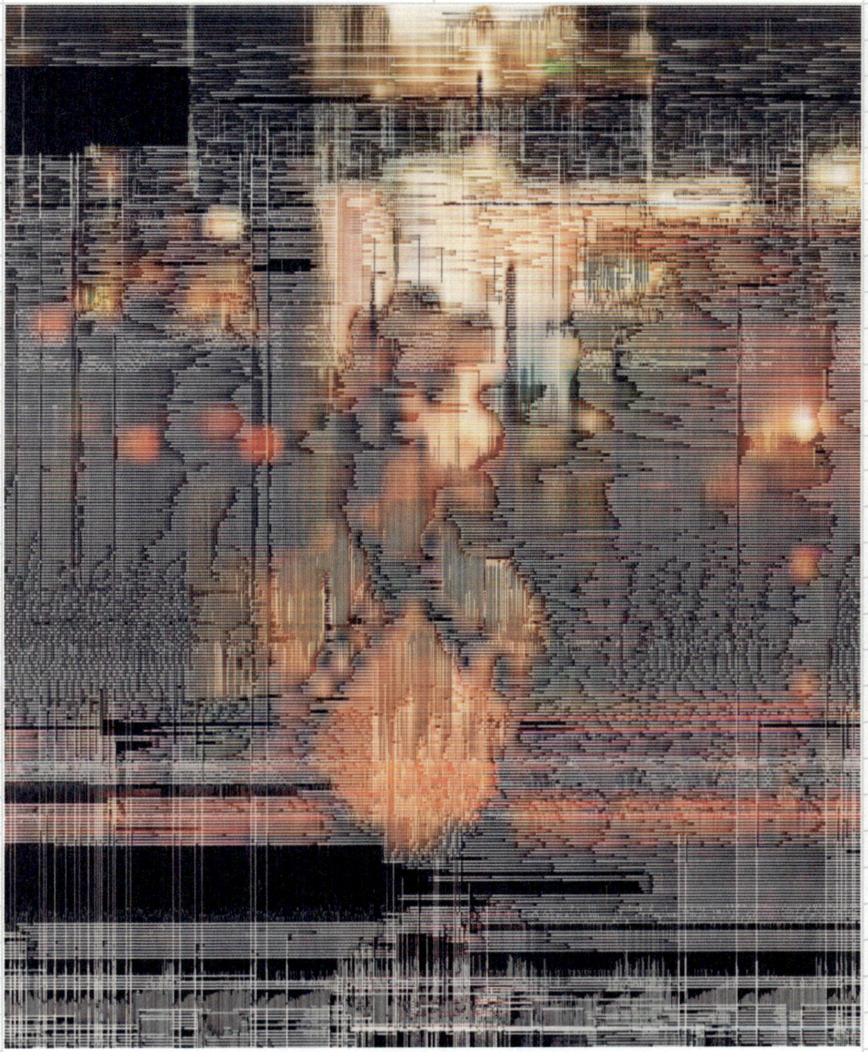

in friction things become clearer and the danger of them escaping, is what makes them more desirable.

enFont Terrible

enFont Terrible was developed by Javier Arce to create and manipulate typefaces. Users can upload fonts from their desktop and change them using sliders to adjust parameters such as the height, width, and thickness of the letters. In addition, five effects can be applied: Rotator rotates letters around their anchor points; Zigzag distorts letters horizontally; Wave applies vertical distortions to create wave-like structures; Pendulum tilts letters at varying angles; and the Boing-Boing effect makes letters jump to different heights.

The interface is deliberately limited to these few functions. Changes are visualized in real time, and the results can be exported as complete OTF files. enFont Terrible is aimed at those interested in experimenting with typography and creating unconventional letter forms without necessarily needing in-depth knowledge of type design software.

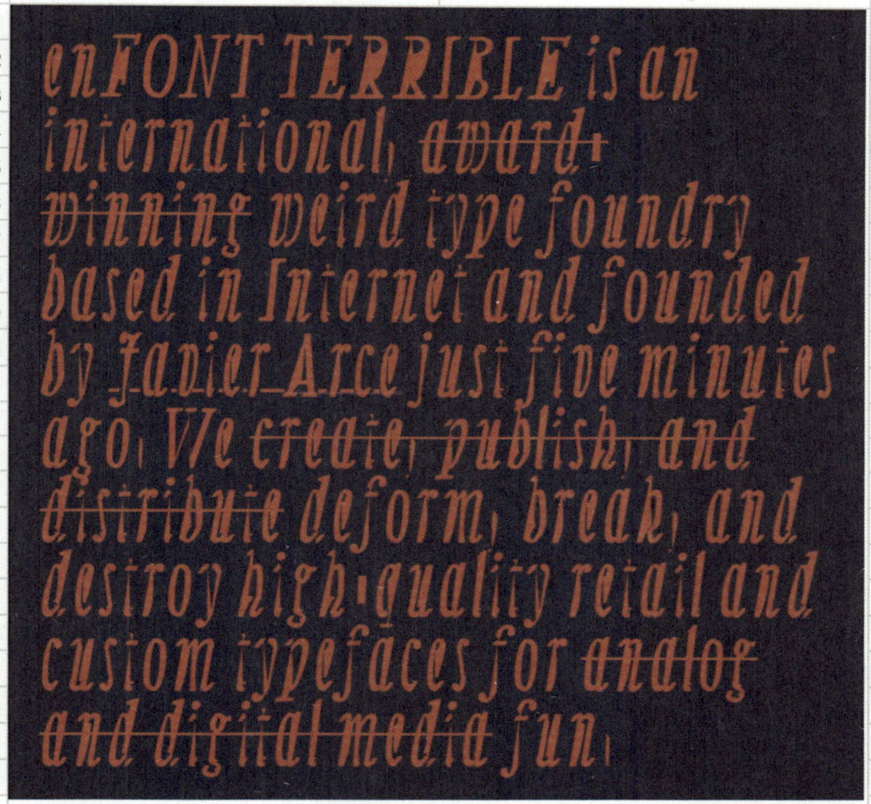

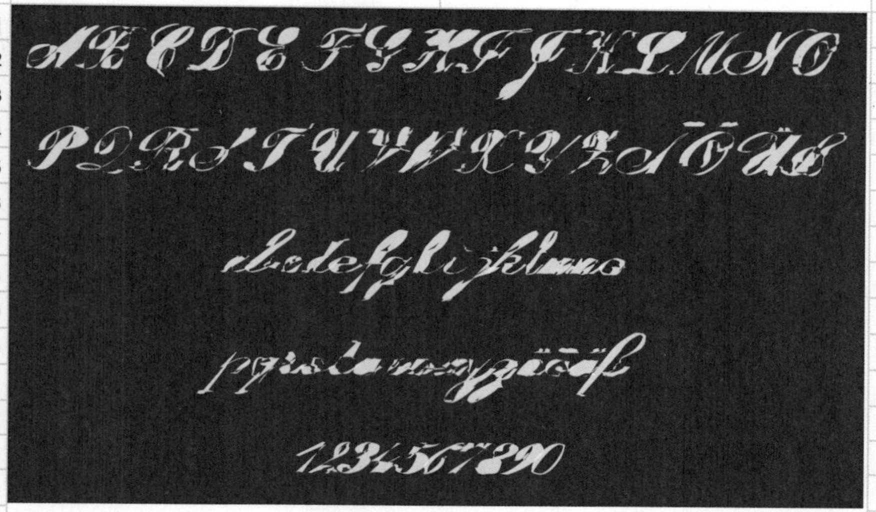

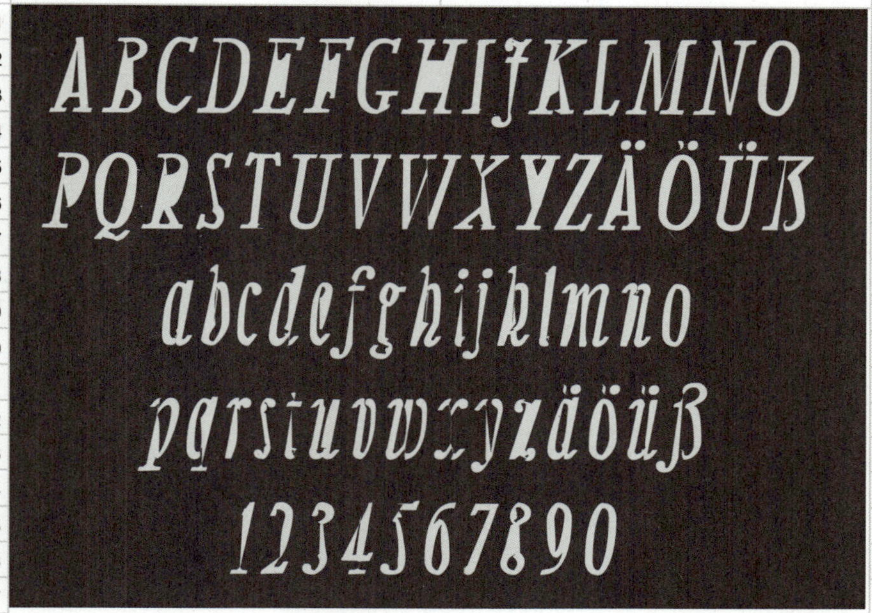
ABCDEFGHIJKLMNO
PQRSTUVWXYZÄÖÜß
abcdefghijklmno
pqrstuvwxyzäöüß
1234567890

deconstruct to
reconstruct
its purpose

Terrible

Kid Pix

Developed in 1989 by Craig Hickman, Kid Pix is a computer program designed specifically for children. It features a colorful user interface with tools such as brushes, stamps, “magic tools”, and sound effects that accompany every action. The program allows painting, drawing, and the creation of simple animations. With its intuitive design and playful approach, Kid Pix was intended to make digital media accessible and fun, encouraging creativity without focusing on technical precision. The icon-based interface, which in its basic structure resembles professional design software, makes it easy to recognize and use tools. Kid Pix became widely known as one of the first creative software environments tailored to children, and has been released in various updated versions over the years.

Sandspiel

Sandspiel is a browser-based sandbox simulation game developed by Max Bittker and released in late 2018. It allows users to place materials such as sand, water, fire, gas, or plants in a pixel-based grid. Each substance interacts based on its own physical properties, resulting in realistic outcomes such as combustion, evaporation, or growth.

The user interface is kept minimalistic. It offers a palette of materials and a few adjustable settings that can be selected with a single click. Sandspiel provides a creative space for experimentation, pattern-making, and exploration of interactions between elements. Its playful and visual approach makes it equally suited for entertainment and creative exploration.

Max Bittker created Sandspiel as an homage to classic “falling sand” games and the micro-communities that emerged around them—such as the Powder Game by dan-ball.jp. He designed Sandspiel not just as a simulation but as a participatory creative environment. It comprises a gallery system where users can upload and browse creations, which fosters a communal and visual form of play.

Sandspiel was initially fascinating thanks to its vivid colors and aesthetic qualities, as well as the option to pause interactions. Elements could be placed statically before being released to react in accordance with their specific properties. The game quickly turned out to be an unusual drawing tool that could also generate animations. Upon further exploration, my focus shifted toward hidden spheres of action beyond the visible interface. Interfaces typically present only those functions intended for users, while additional structures often exist in the background. By systematically testing and probing the system, you can search for such hidden potentials, by inserting text onto the canvas, for instance, by dragging and dropping images, or by using Chrome Developer Tools to access the underlying code.

I discovered by chance that SVG files

could be pasted directly from the clipboard onto the canvas. This made it possible to integrate any design created in an SVG editor. Sandspiel automatically translates these graphics into game elements, based on contrasts and colors. The resulting outputs can be saved or animated, transforming the tool into both an aesthetic filter and a generator for motion-based compositions.

Friction
initiates
movement;
without
movement,
there remains
a state of
stagnation

If you have a ball, you throw it; if you have a chair, you sit on it. But digital devices are characterized by the fact that regardless of the function, you treat them the same way. Interaction gets trimmed down to ur fingertips

pervasive
com-
puting
is the
norm

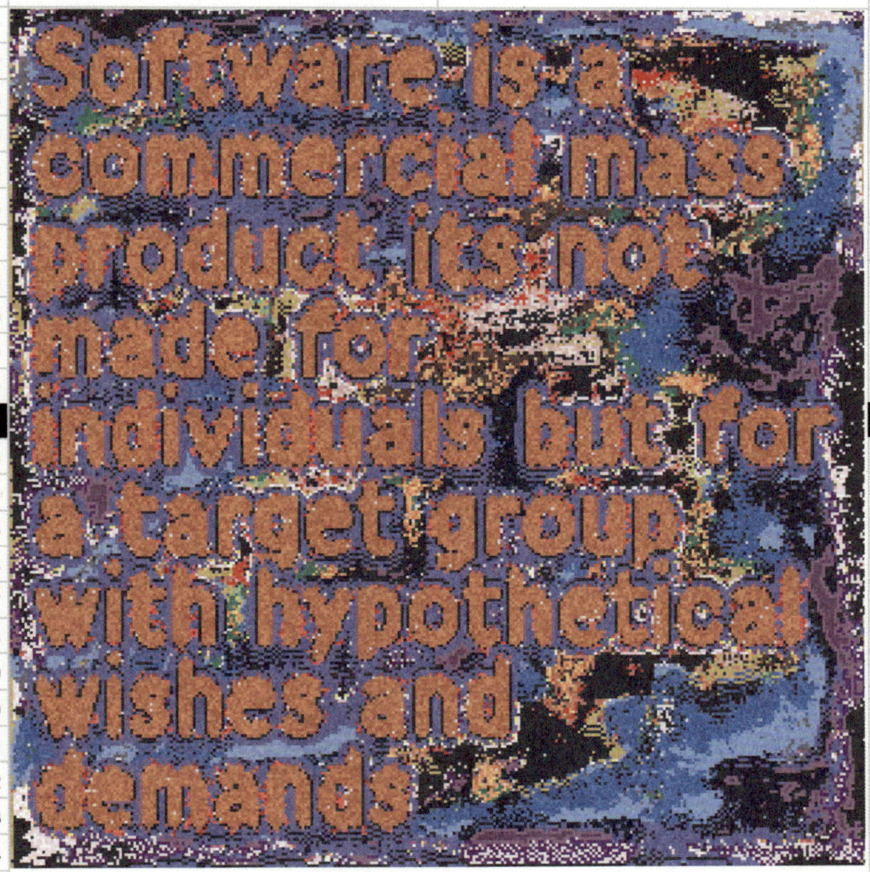
Software is a
commercial mass
product its not
made for
individuals but for
a target group
with hypothetical
wishes and
demands

Adapt
To
the workflow
ØR GET

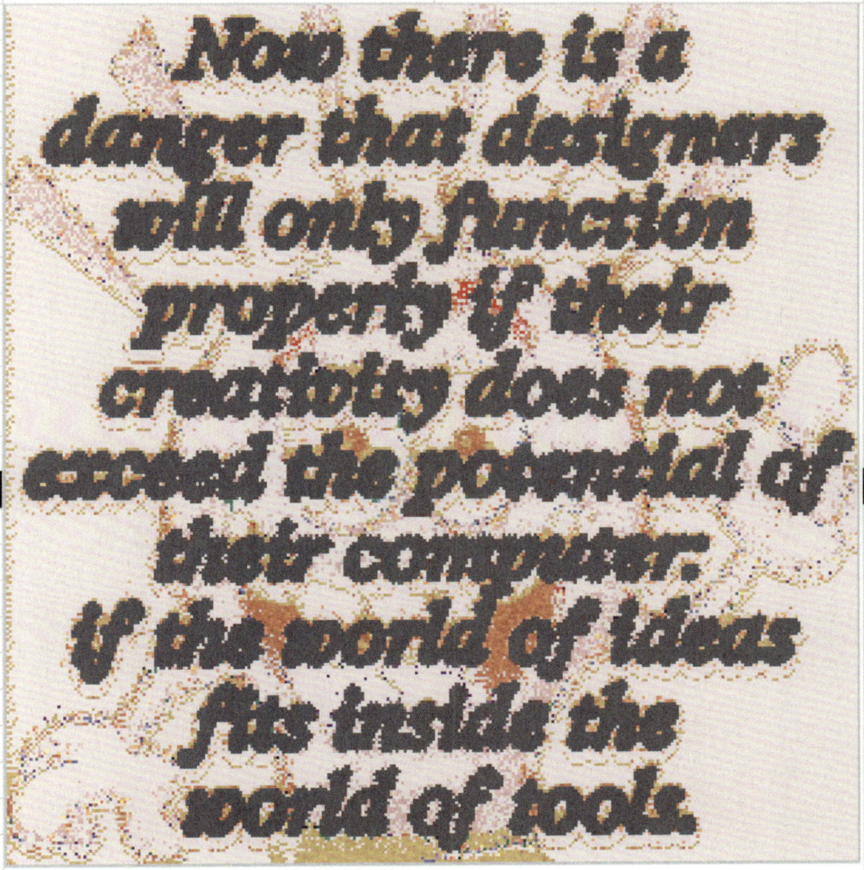
Now there is a
danger that designers
will only function
properly if their
creativity does not
exceed the potential of
their computer.
If the world of ideas
fits inside the
world of tools.

If all you
have is a
hammer,
everything
looks like
a nail.

Making tools
smarter also
means taking
decisions away
from the
designer

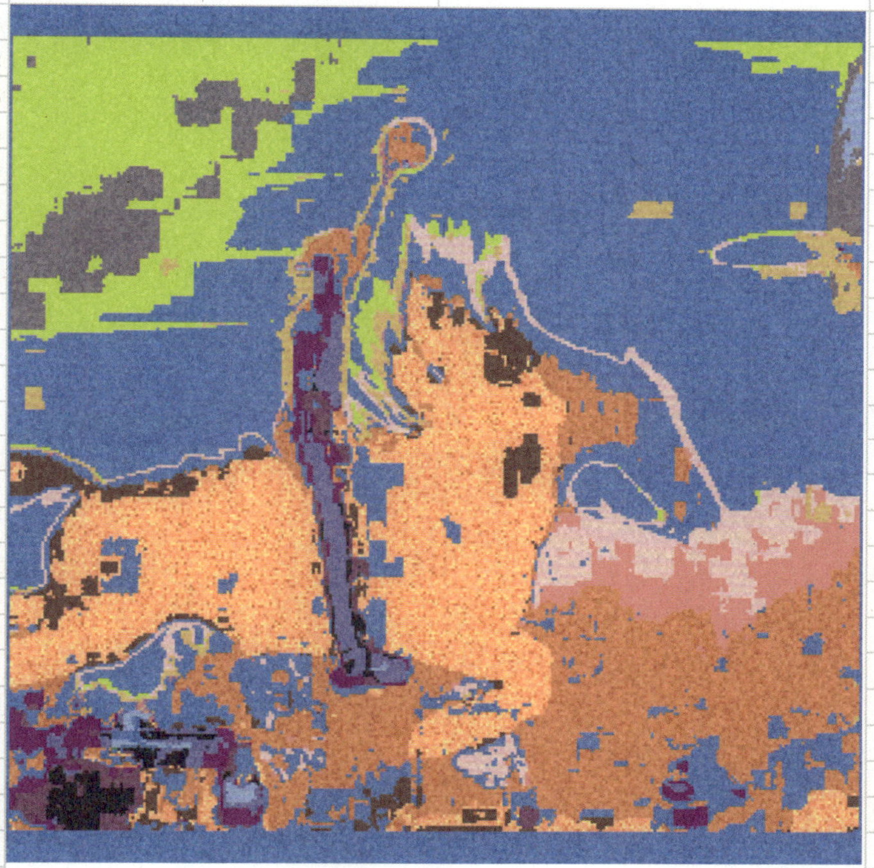

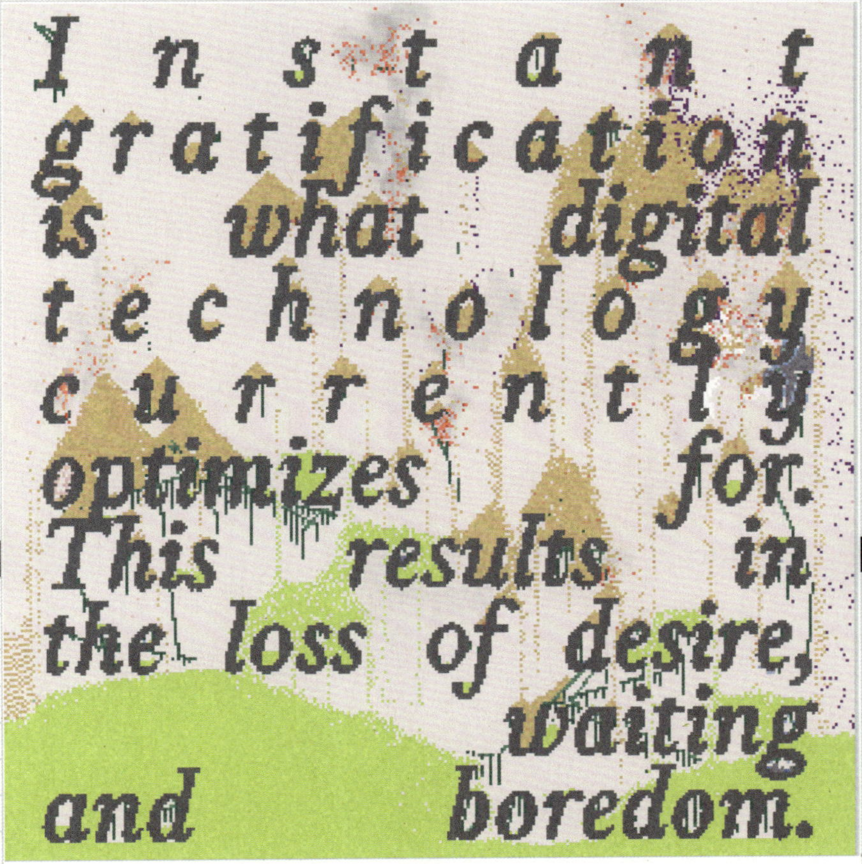
Instant gratification is what digital technology currently optimizes for. This results in the loss of desire, waiting and boredom.

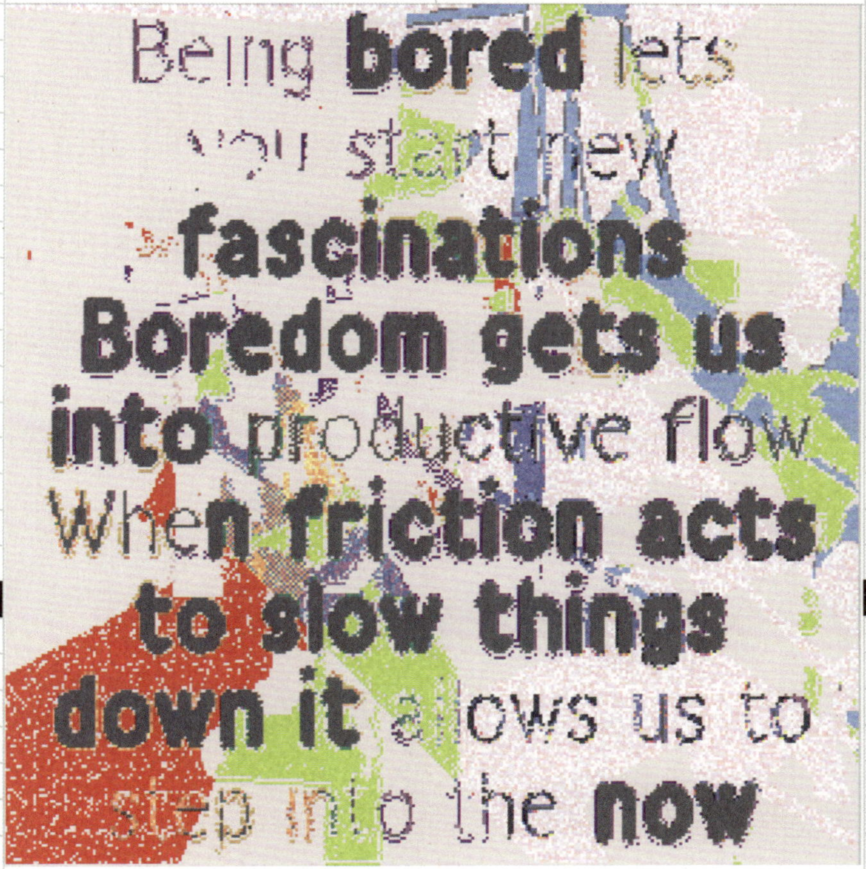
Being bored lets
you start new
fascinations
Boredom gets us
into productive flow
When friction acts
to slow things
down it allows us to
step into the now

Human
messiness
counteracts
the goal of
prediction.

Ouroborus

Ouroborus is a browser-based tool developed by DIA Studio as an experimental platform for self-referential shaders. It generates recursive feedback loops in real time and allows users to create animations and visual effects based on text input. The interface consists of a live preview and a dropdown menu with sliders to adjust various settings. The tool offers a selection of presets as well as a randomization function, enabling you to explore different combinations quickly and easily. Ouroborus makes experimenting with cyclical and infinite-loop aesthetics accessible, drawing inspiration from the symbolic idea of the ouroboros—the serpent devouring its own tail. DIA Studio is a branding and graphic design studio based in New York City and Chamonix, France, specializing in kinetic identities and typographic systems (tools.dia.tv). Ouroborus is part of their online TOOLS archive, a growing library of interactive research tools intended to provide immersive access to their experimental tests.

This tool
hurts
the eyes

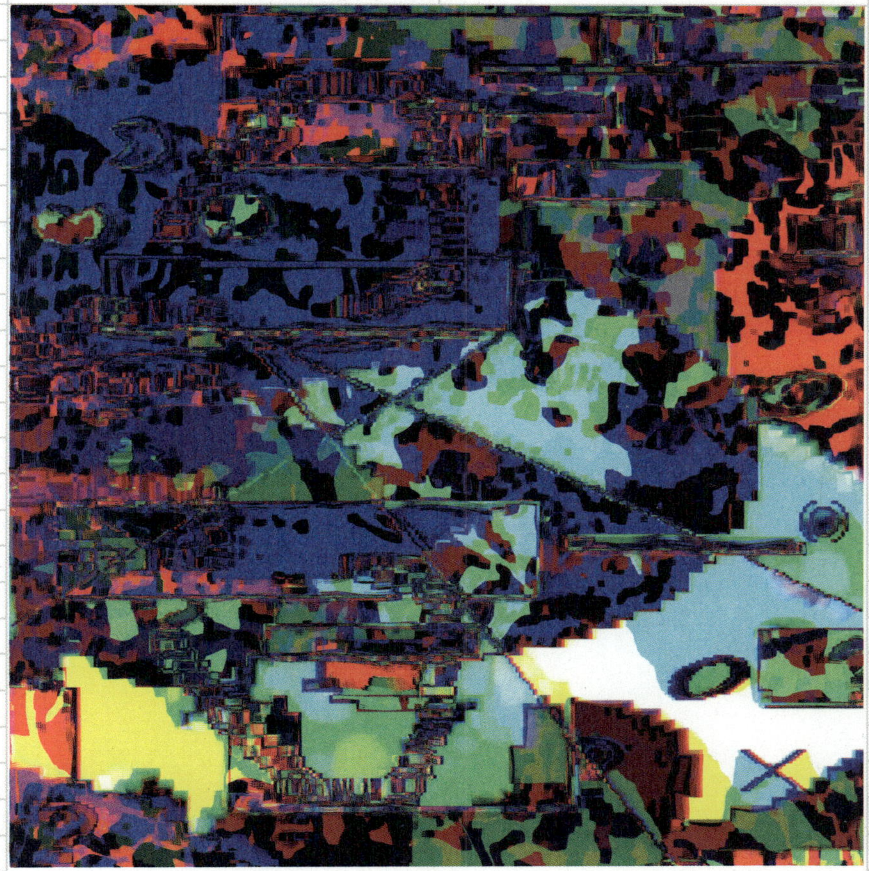

Gubernat Tool 1

This tool by Florian Gubernator enables highly limited creation of pixel graphics. The interface provides four fixed colors that cannot be changed, plus two sliders. One slider adjusts the size of the pixels being edited, while the other controls the random redistribution of the pixel arrangement. In addition, there is a function for generating a new random variation based on the two selected parameters and the predefined options.

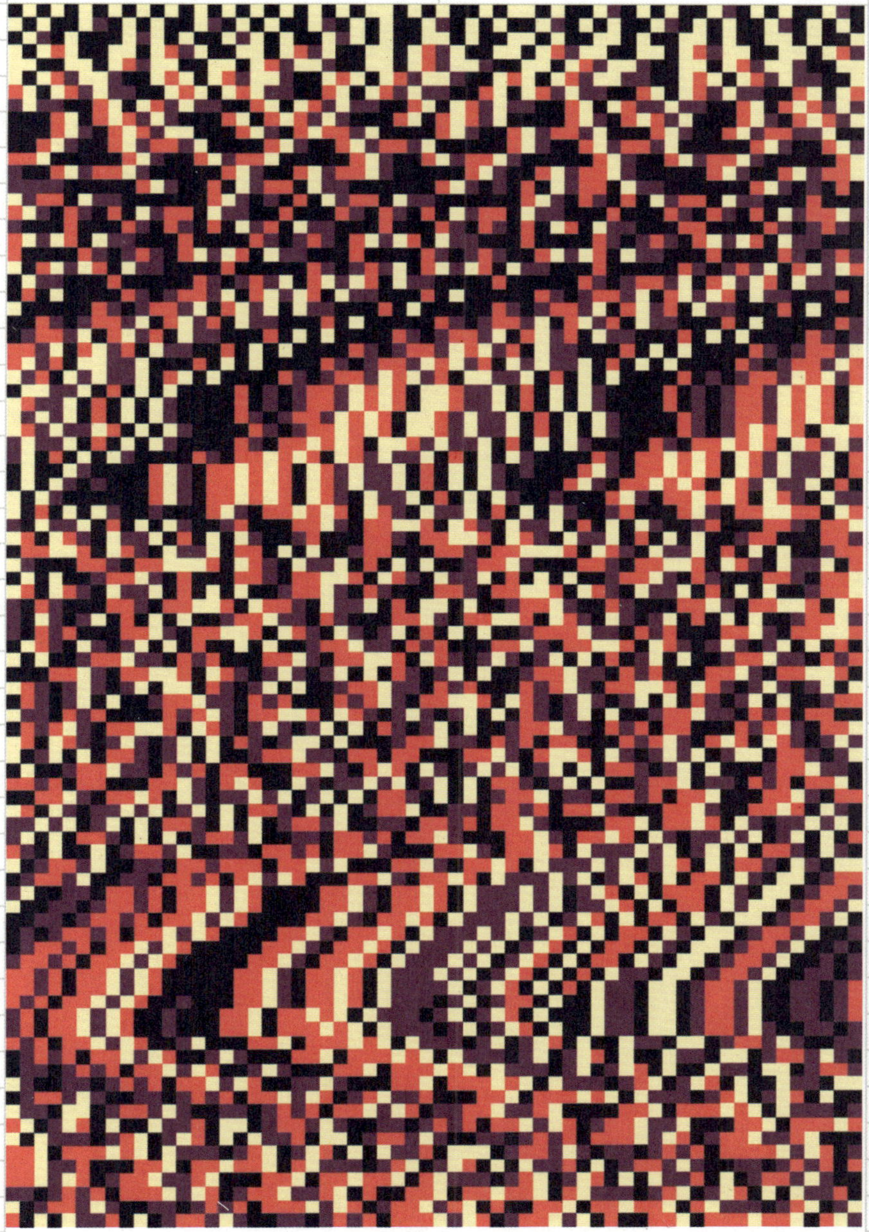

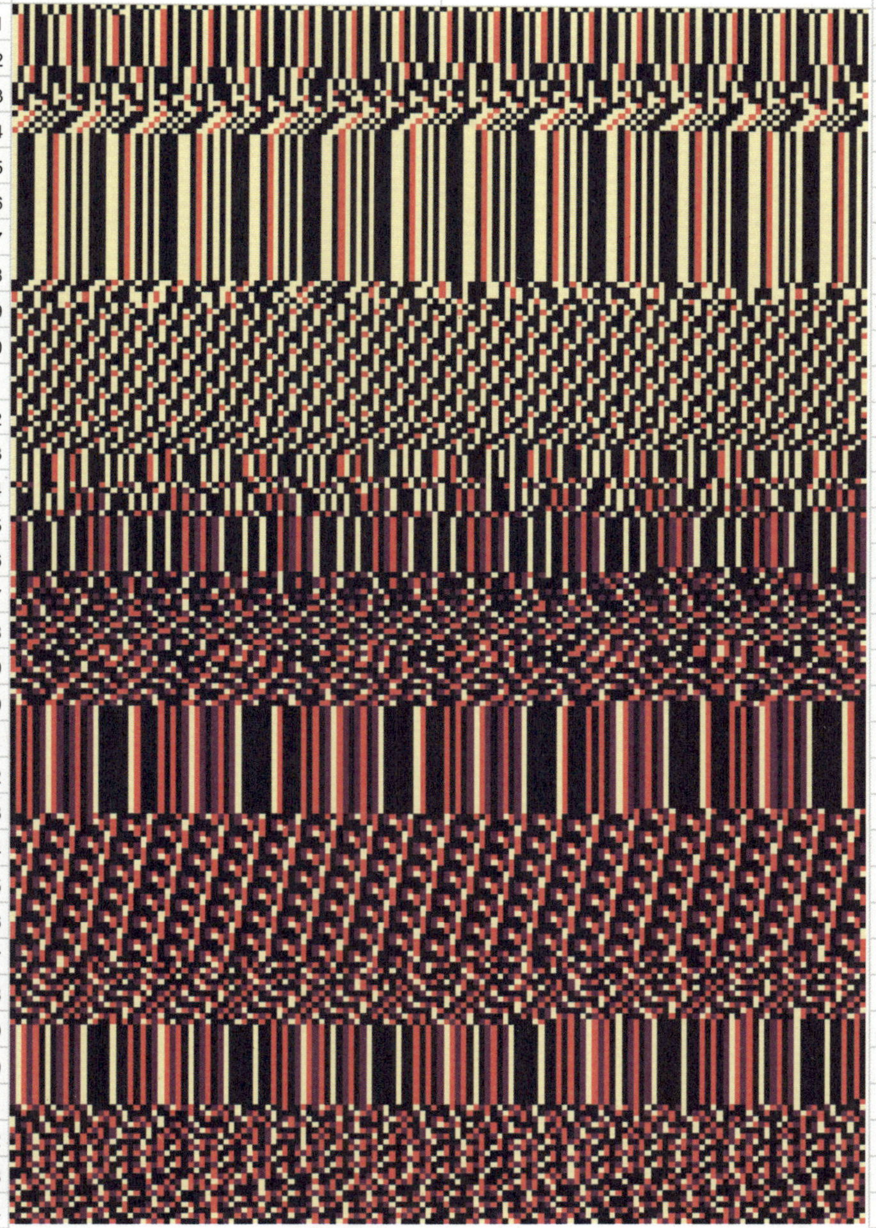

Page 104 | Anti-Environments

Page 105 | Gubernat Tool 1

Mosaic Tool

Mosaic is an open-source tool from the Constraint Systems collection that reconstructs one image using portions of another. The tool divides the source image into square tiles and rearranges them based on contrast similarity to the target image, effectively reassembling the uploaded image. The interface is minimalistic, offering only two upload fields—one for each image—and a button to switch their roles. The transformation process begins automatically as soon as both images have been uploaded and processed. Constraint Systems is a collection of experimental, web-based creative tools exploring alternative interfaces for editing and creating images and text.

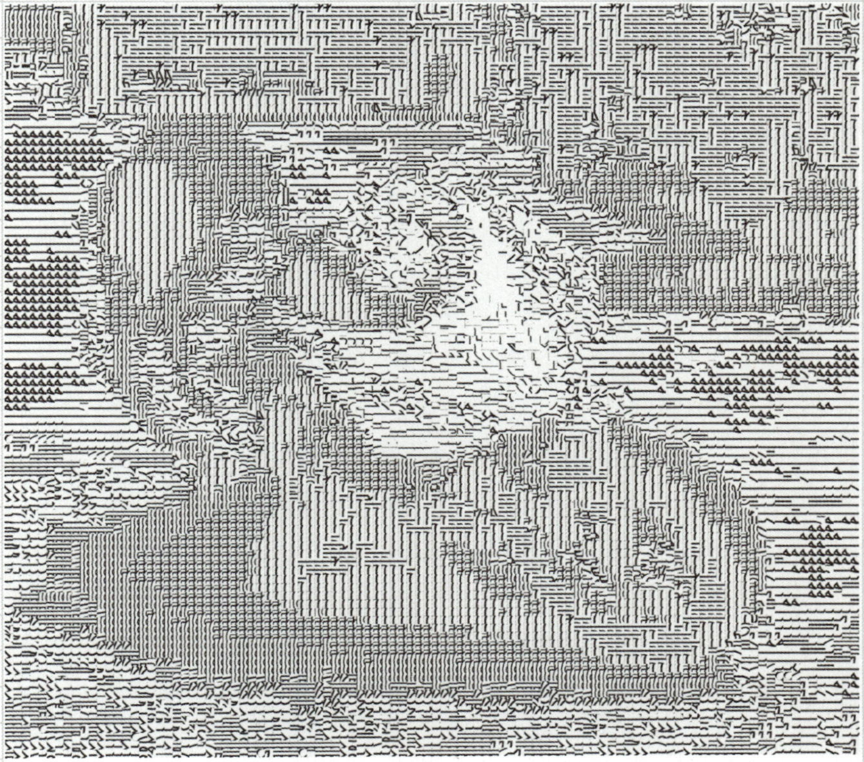

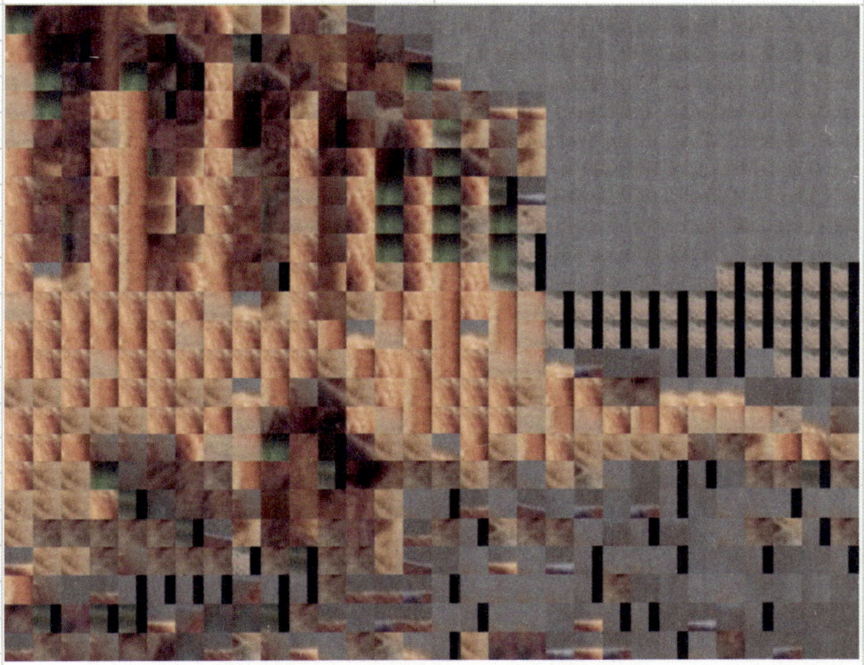

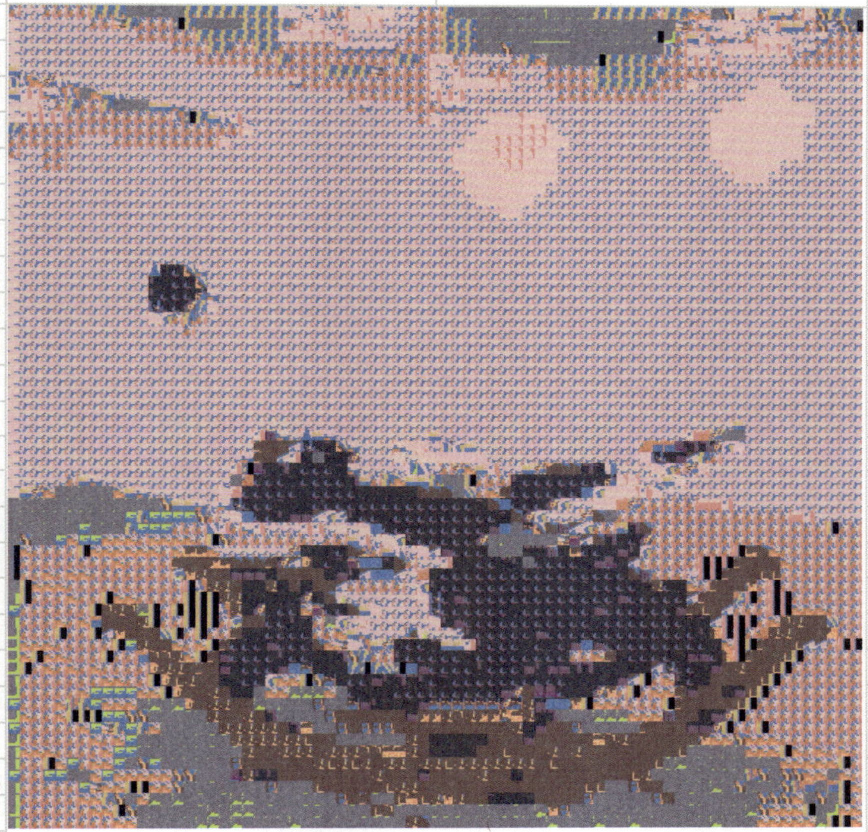

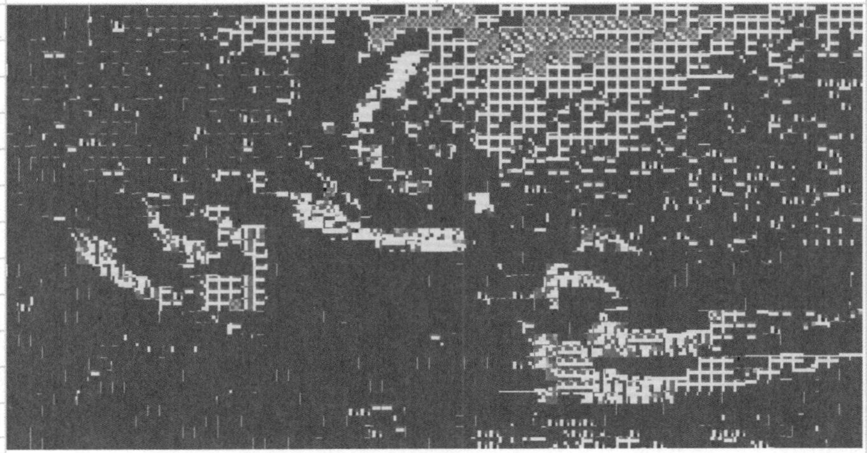

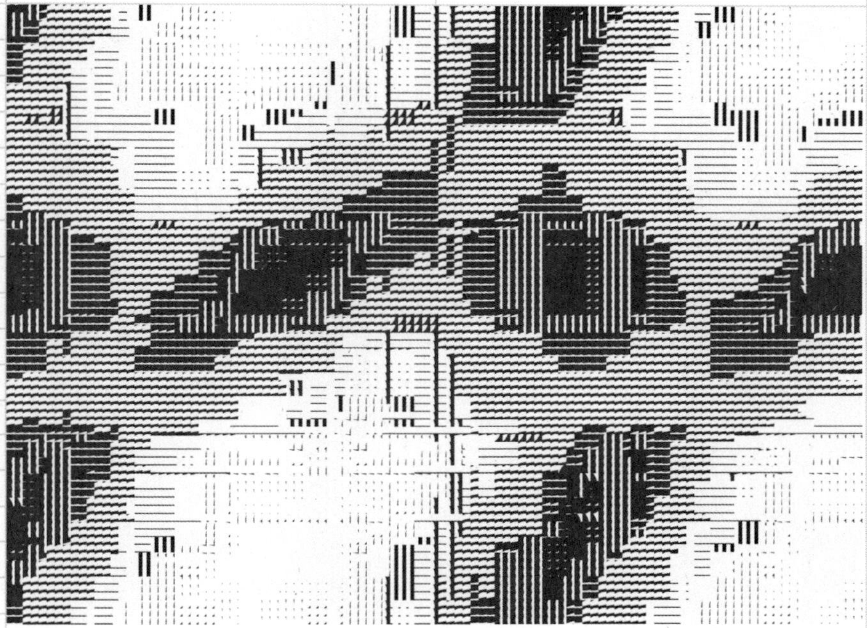

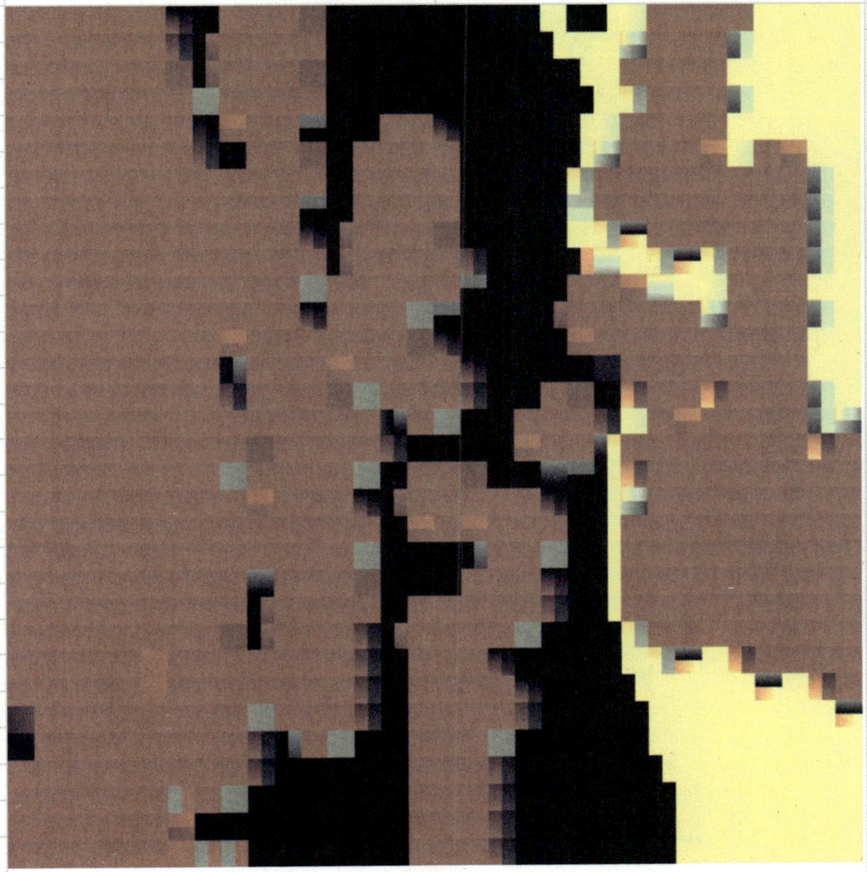

Google Sheets

Google Sheets is Google's own cloud-based spreadsheet software and part of Google Workspace. The program enables you to create and edit spreadsheets directly in the browser without having to install anything. The interface consists of a grid view with cells for data entry, along with toolbars for functions such as formatting, chart creation, and data analysis. Users can collaborate in real time, track changes, and manage sharing permissions.

Unlike traditional desktop-based spreadsheet programs such as Microsoft Excel, Google Sheets emphasizes accessibility through the cloud and seamless multi-user collaboration. It also supports functions, scripts, and integrations with other Google services, making it suitable for data organization, calculations, and collaborative projects.

Google Sheets proved to be one of the most central tools in the project, not just because of its immediate design options, but, above all, due to the potential its repurposing—or subversion—as a publishing environment revealed. First, our attention was drawn to the grid, which, through simple color blocking, could be used as a pixel grid for drawings and visual experiments. In addition, we were able to use App Script extensions to define algorithmic parameters that generated abstract compositions. More complex scripts resulted in glitches, collapsing grids, and unexpected geometric skewing. In this context, things that would normally be considered errors became aesthetic design moments. Even more significant was the possibility of using Google Sheets as a publication medium. Unlike when content is designed in specialized

tools such as InDesign, subverting a big-tech tool created an opportunity to develop a web-to-print system that is directly available, collaborative, shareable, and printable, regardless of the original intent of authoritarian corporations. Here, subversion becomes a strategy for moving out of a marginalized position in a power structure. It allows us to send a signal of resistance and also regain autonomy. At the same time, this approach shows that digital tools we have had access to for a long time contain much greater potential than their official scope of application would suggest. The question is whether we always need new, specialized tools, or if should we examine existing systems in more depth to discover hidden possibilities. If you work in InDesign, you almost inevitably find yourself conforming to its visual standards. Google Sheets,

on the other hand, forces you to question those standards. Many decisions made in this environment during the project would not have been made—or would not have been able to be made—in a classical layout program. The lack of pre-existing solutions opened up a freedom between limitation, friction, and compromise, while underlining a new responsibility: to examine the system ourselves, to shape it, and to adapt it for design purposes. It is precisely in this resulting otherness that the potential lies. Instead of imitating the logic of conventional tools, Google Sheets' own aesthetic was taken seriously. The result was a book with a layout and body that are not only technically feasible, but also embody a conceptual statement—a book that itself reveals and highlights the structures' underlying design.

CREATE SITUATIONS THAT ARE NOT PREDICTED, MEASURED AND CALCULATED BEFOREHAND SITUATIONS THAT RESULT FROM AND AMOUNT TO THE PRESENT MOMENT.

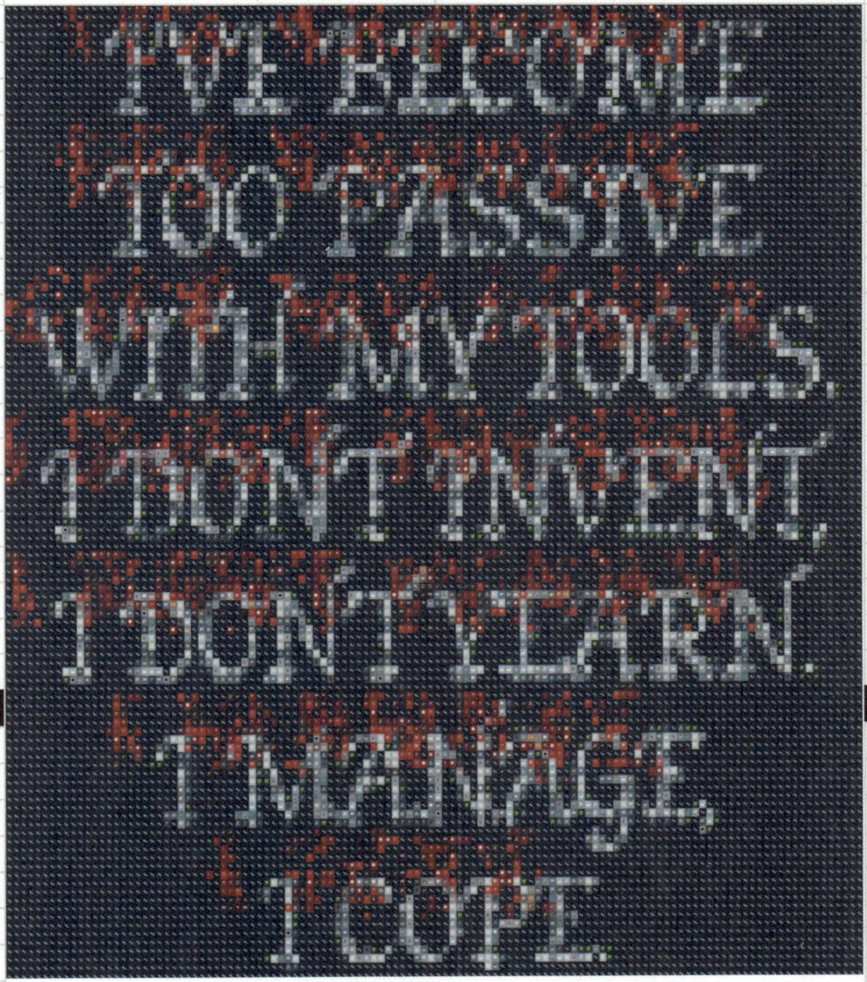
I'VE BECOME
TOO PASSIVE
WITH MY TOOLS.
I DON'T INVENT,
I DON'T LEARN.
I MANAGE,
I COPE.

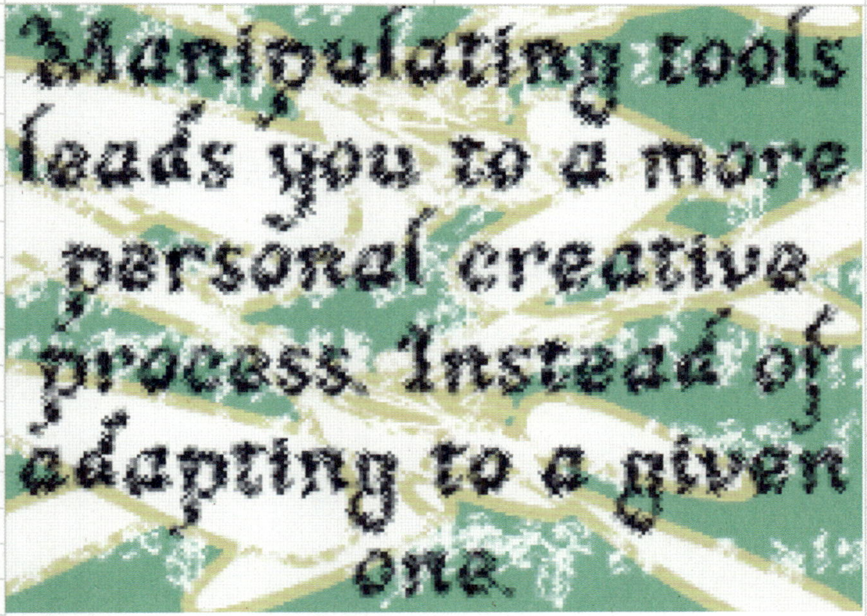
Manipulating tools
leads you to a more
personal creative
process. Instead of
adapting to a given
one.

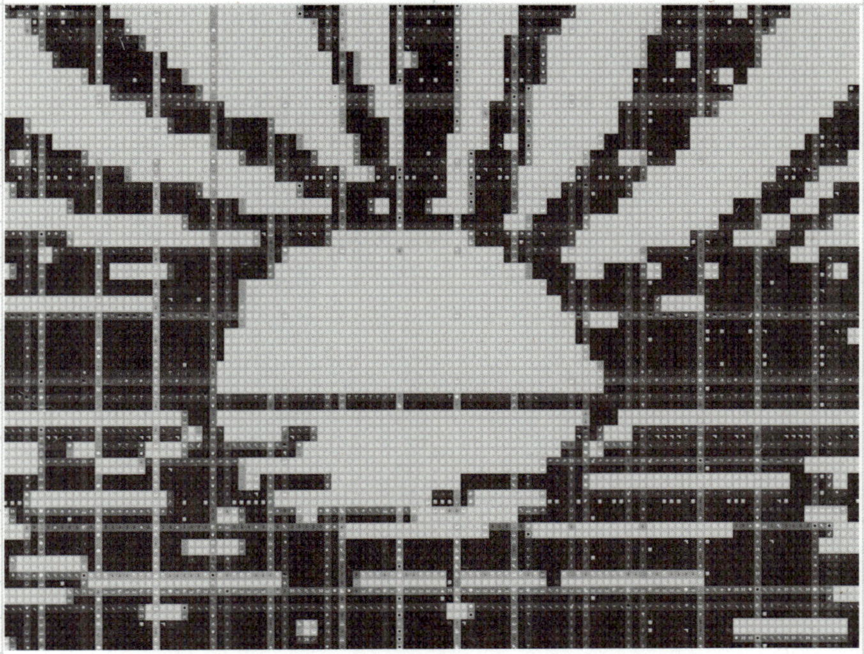

Overload
the grid
move the
cursor
wild

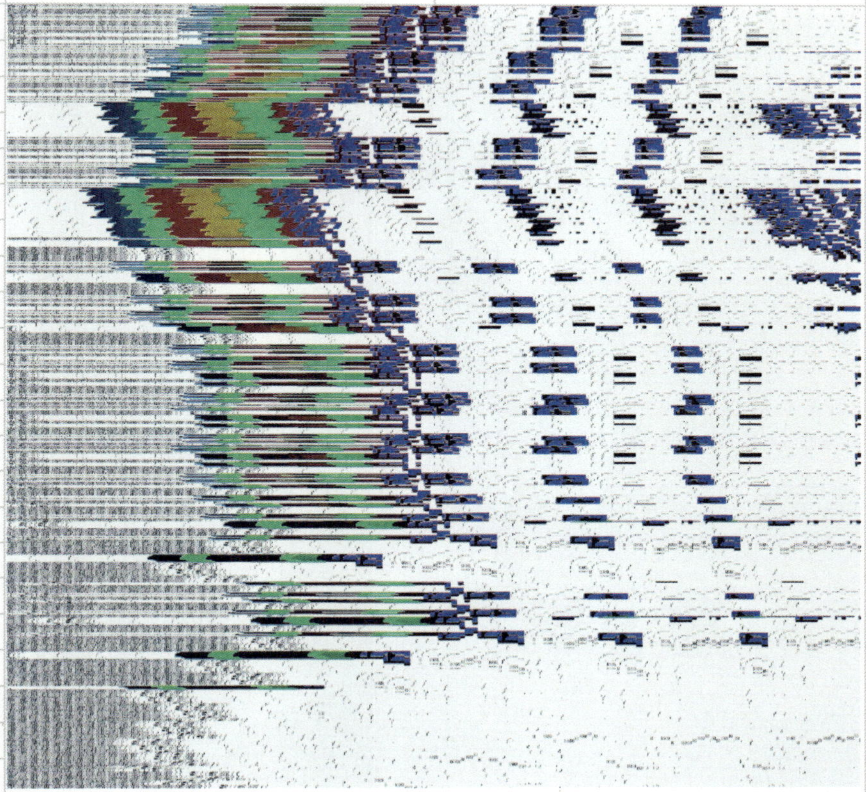

Another offering by Florian Gubernator, Gubernat Tool 2, allows you to display and transform text on a surface. Users can enter text and adjust parameters such as font size, precision, and probability. They can also change the color of the background and text. What distinguishes this tool is the reconfiguration of letter, word, and sentence structures. Letters are distorted, shifted, and rearranged, pushing the conventional reading process to its limits. Depending on the probability and precision settings, results range from easily legible texts to abstract, graphic compositions. Control over the process is deliberately limited, which fosters an exploratory approach that resists strict obedience to the tool itself.

Gubernat Tool 2

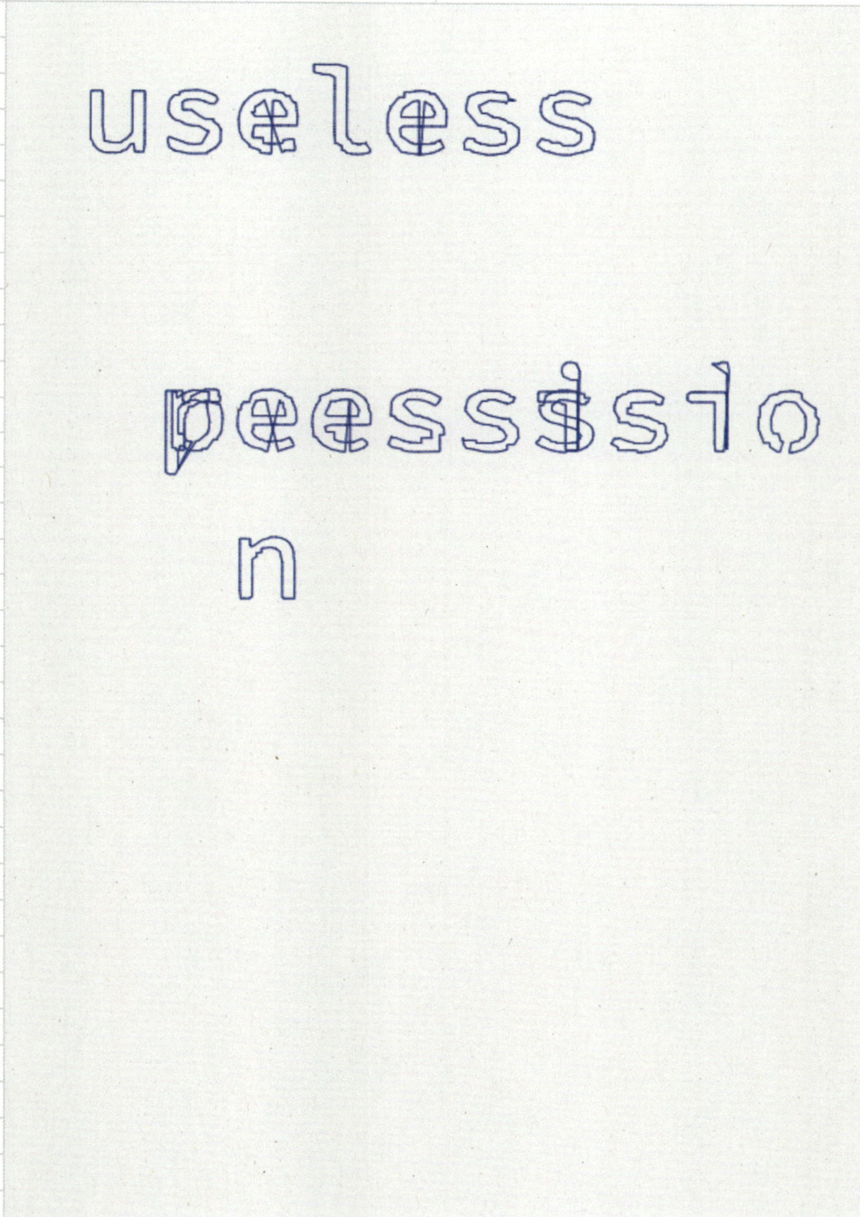

Tools

that

serve

no

purpo se

poetic explorrat

ons o

n

w techbogy

can

resul

fro

pshhiing

ns a set of

ogcal

osttrains

iinadggwoksginningist

r

intterfffa

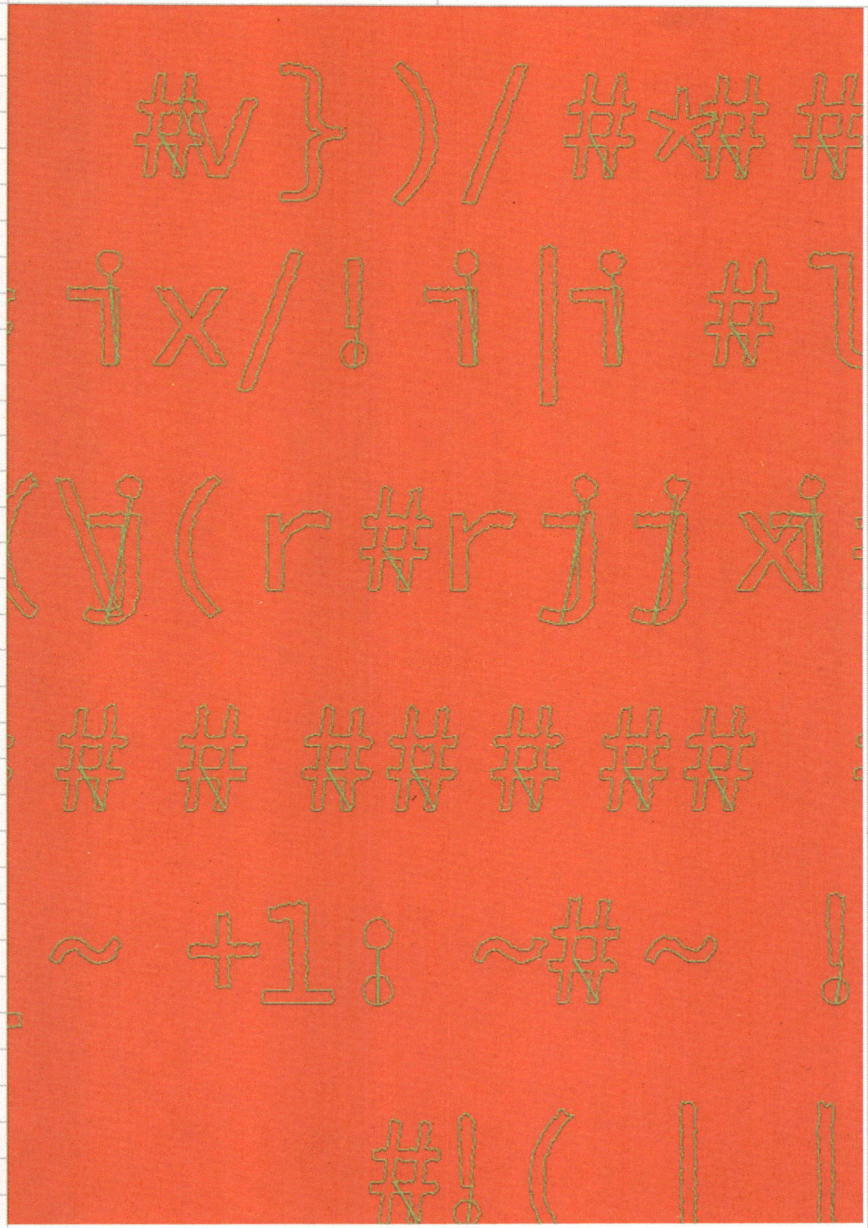

Hex Tool

Hex is a keyboard-controlled, grid-based drawing tool from the Constraint Systems collection. Drawing is done exclusively via keyboard input. Four arrow keys determine direction, while five additional keys assign different line types—each corresponding to one side of a hexagon.

To erase, users must activate delete mode and press the corresponding key on each grid cell individually. There is no fast option to undo or redo steps. Hex deliberately slows down the creative process compared to conventional touchpad- or mouse-based drawing tools. This aligns with the broader ethos of Constraint Systems, where built-in limitations are used to shift the focus from detailed control to experimental, exploratory creation.

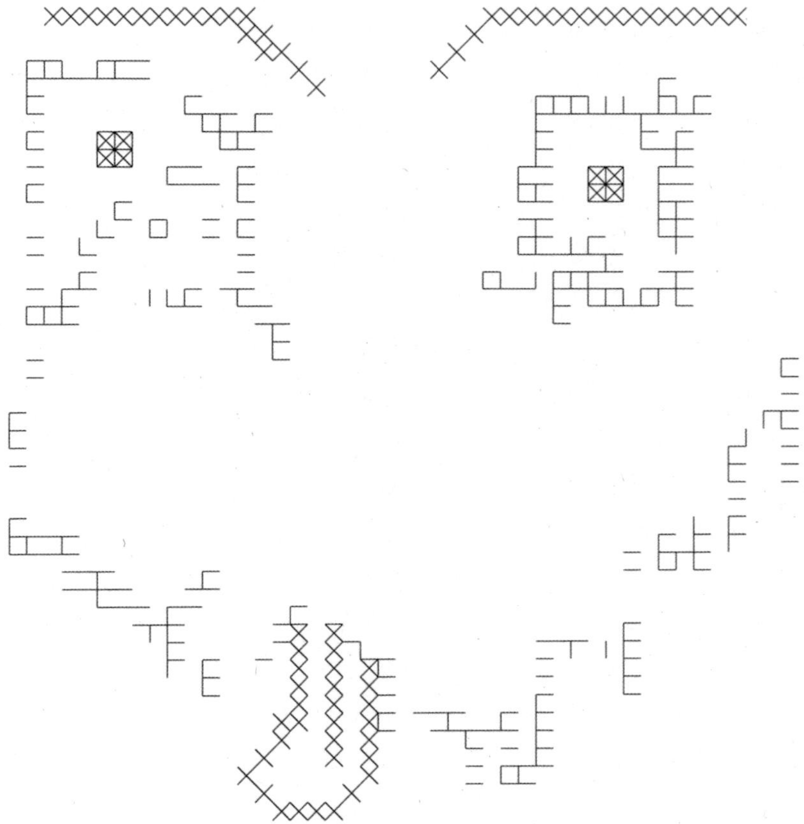

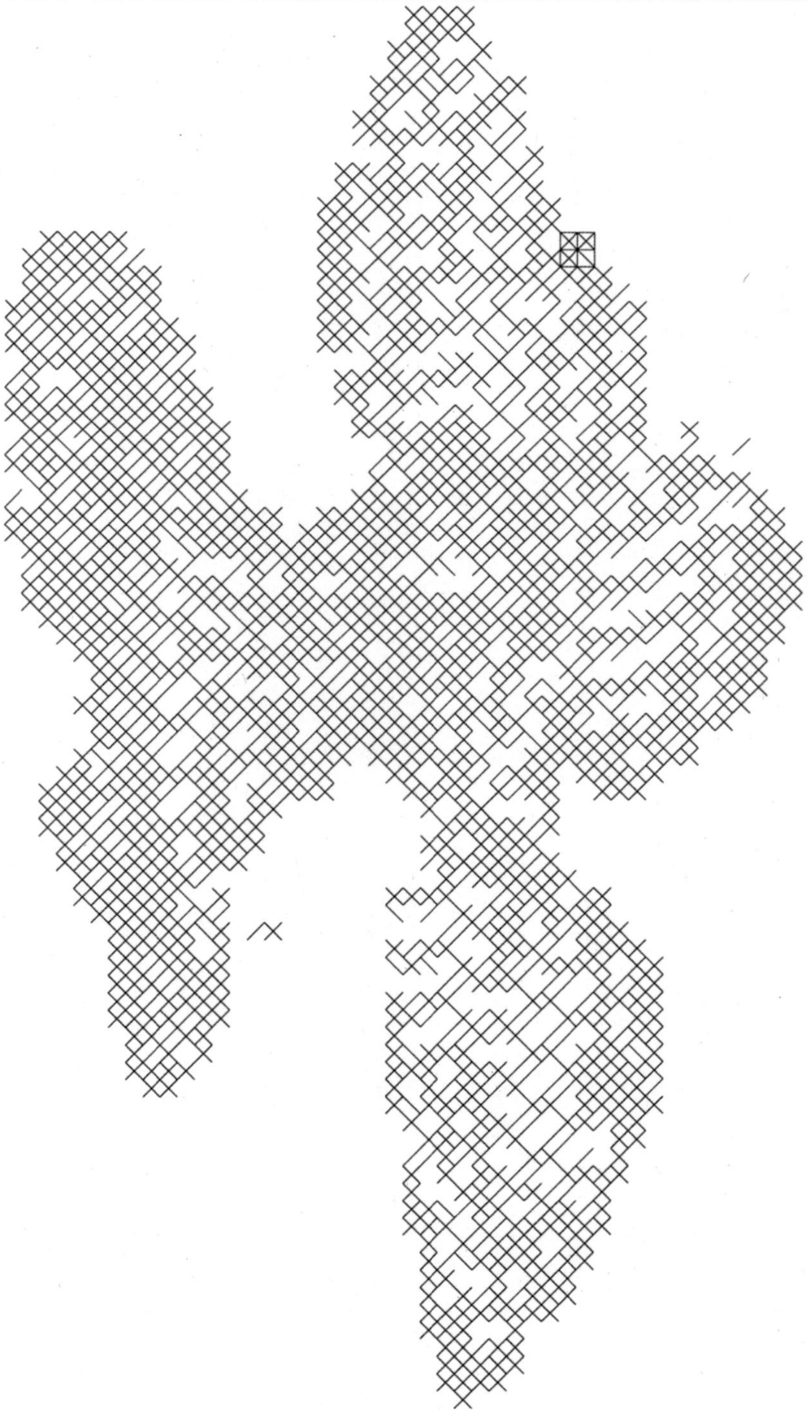

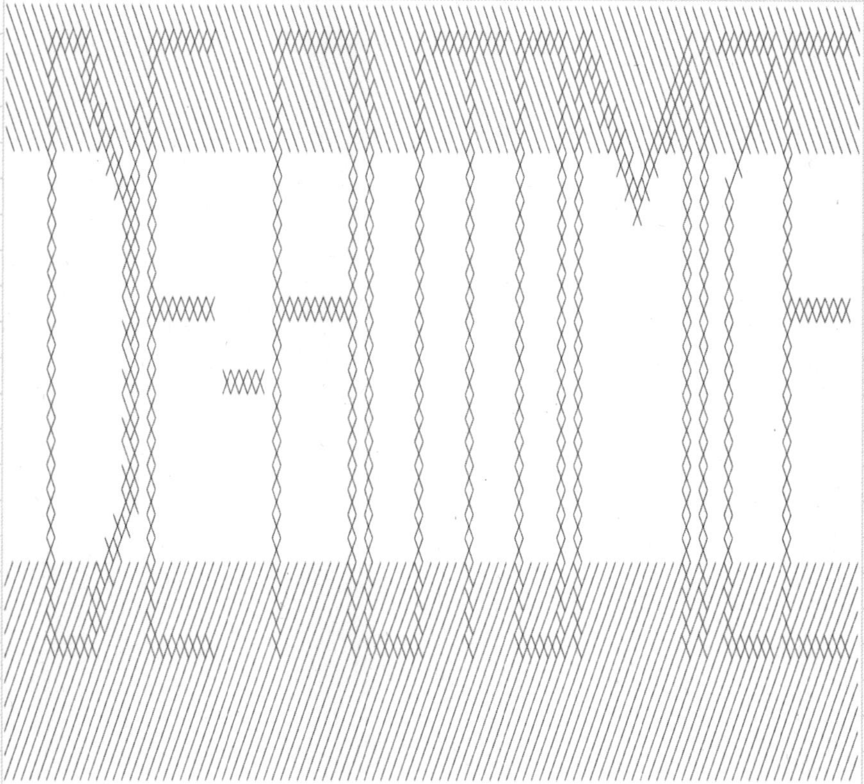

Gradientor by Anatoly Grashchenko is a tool for drawing with color gradients. The interface is simple, offering options to set the canvas size and select colors for the top, middle, and bottom areas of the gradient. Users can draw directly on the canvas with the defined gradients and use a grain option to add extra texture. It is also possible to upload SVG files, which are then traced within the tool. Finished works can be exported as PNG files. Gradientor makes working with gradients accessible in an unusual way, allowing you to isolate and easily reproduce this specific aesthetic.

Anatoly Grashchenko publishes Gradientor and other experimental, browser-based tools as part of his ongoing exploration of interactive design and generative graphics.

Gradientor

Collage Tool

This tool from the Constraint Systems collection enables you to create a collective collage. The interface displays only the current version of the collage, with the option to download it or upload your own image. When an image is uploaded, it is broken down into individual parts, and only those with the highest pixel complexity are added to the collage. This offers an unusual approach to processing images in accordance with these parameters, resulting in a fragmentary, continuously evolving product.

Constraint Systems is a collection of experimental, web-based creative tools exploring alternative interfaces for editing and creating images and text.

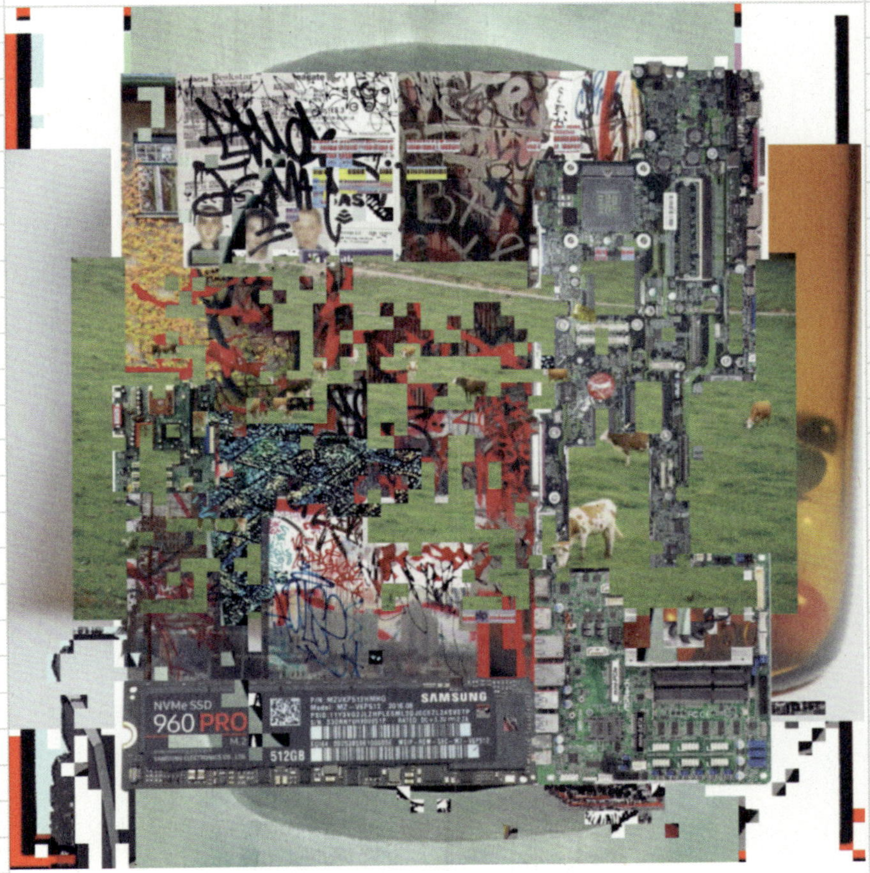
SAMSUNG
NVMe SSD
960 PRO
512GB

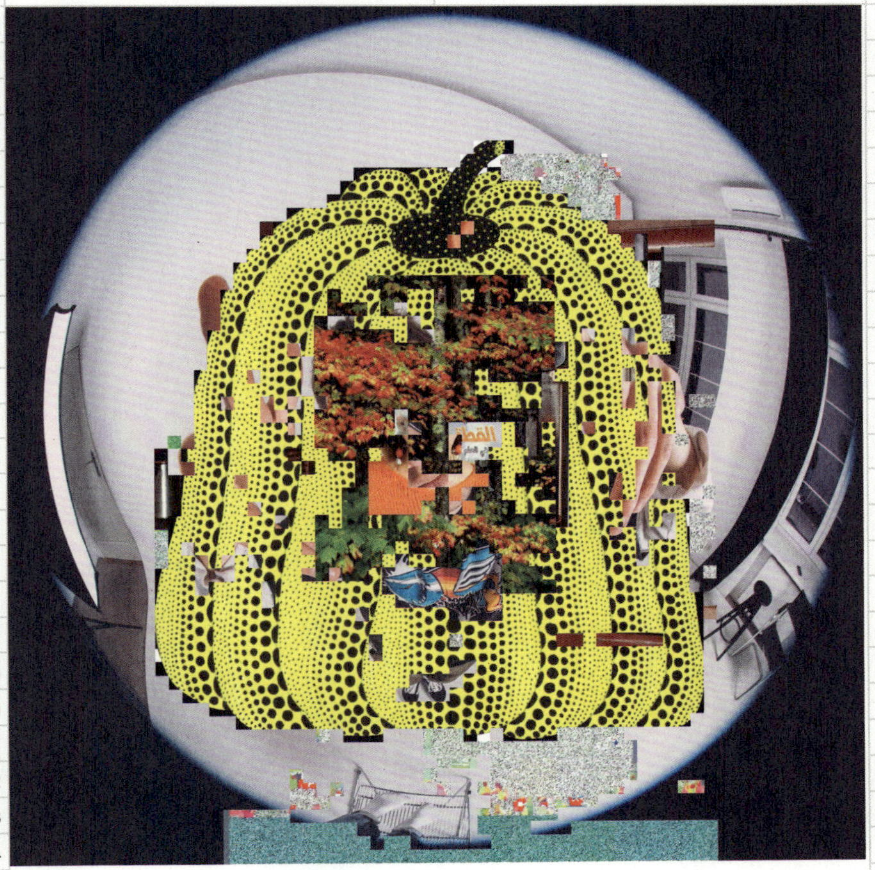

Conservation Tool

Conservation is an unconventional drawing tool from the Constraint Systems collection that explores the relationship between color values and pixel arrangements on a surface. The drawing area is based on a fixed pixel grid, where RGB values are defined via three sliders on the interface. These sliders determine not only the brush color but also the number and distribution of colors across the entire canvas.

Users can invert color settings, randomize them, or enlarge the brush. The limitations of the small pixel grid and the tool's inherent logic mean that outcomes often include unintended effects and dissolving image fragments. Drawing always implies the simultaneous disappearance of existing pixels elsewhere. As a result, the drawing experience is primarily abstract and characterized by chance.

Like other Constraint Systems tools, Conservation employs restrictions and unexpected behaviors as a way to foster experimental and exploratory forms of image-making.

perhaps your
attention
wanders if
there are
no rough
edges

DISRUPT THE
PREVAILING
NARRATIVE
OF CONVENIE-
NCE AT ANY
COST

drawing
in
erasing

Every Shor
t cut you
internalize
tes a
dista
ween

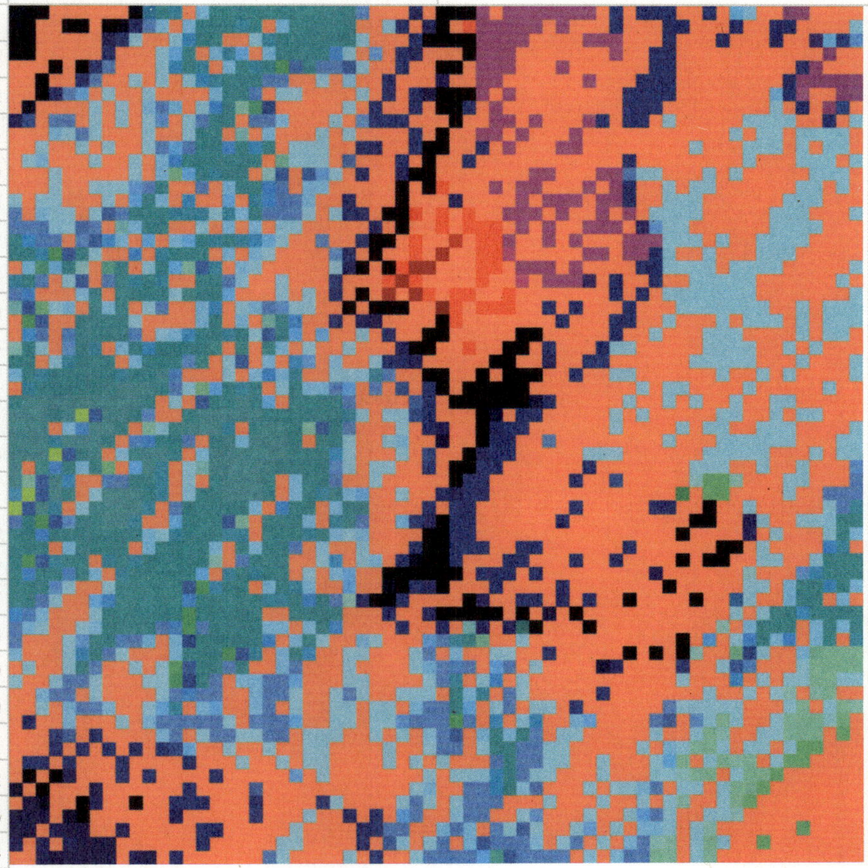

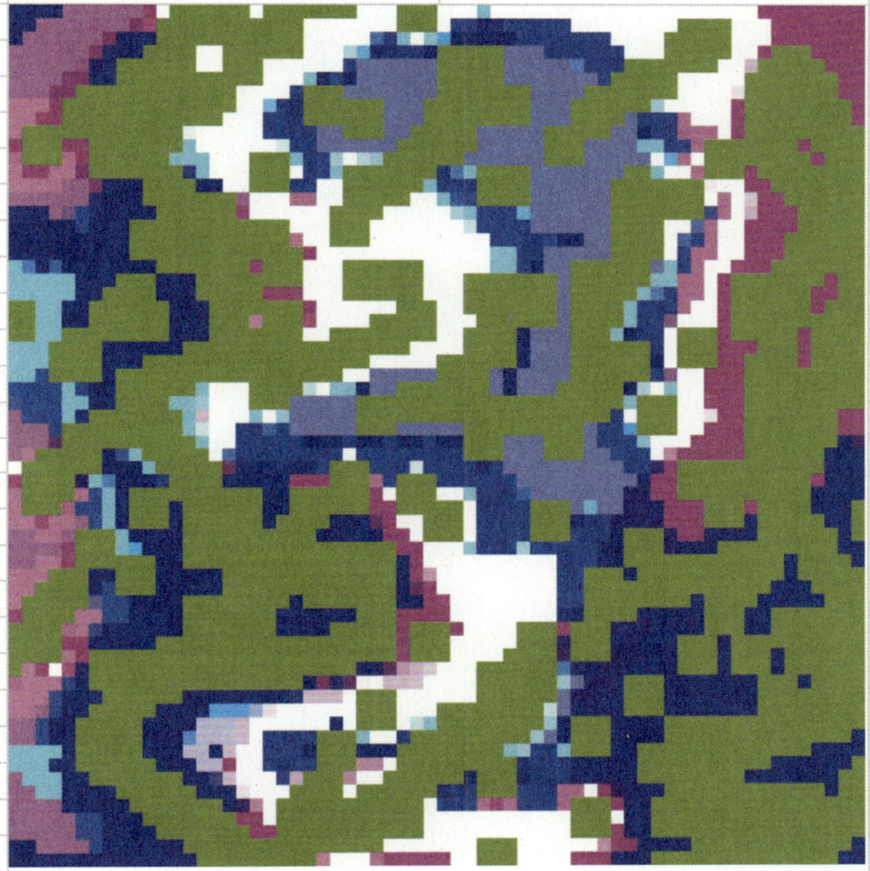

Accordion Tool

Accordion is a tool by DIA Studio that enables you to create dynamic typographic compositions. The interface consists of a live preview and sliders in a dropdown menu that allow you to adjust the grid and the speed of the elements. In addition, the displayed texts can be defined in terms of both content and color across four fields. Users can use the input options to generate animations or feed images, videos, or camera input into the tool.

The tool's strength lies in expanding the accessibility and application of ASCII art principles. Furthermore, by using camera input as a positioning factor for typographic elements, Accordion encourages users to engage more intensely with their own bodies and surroundings when using the tool. As part of DIA Studio's TOOLS archive, Accordion reflects the studio's broader focus on kinetic typography and experimental design systems.

ENGAGE WITH UR WHOLE BODY

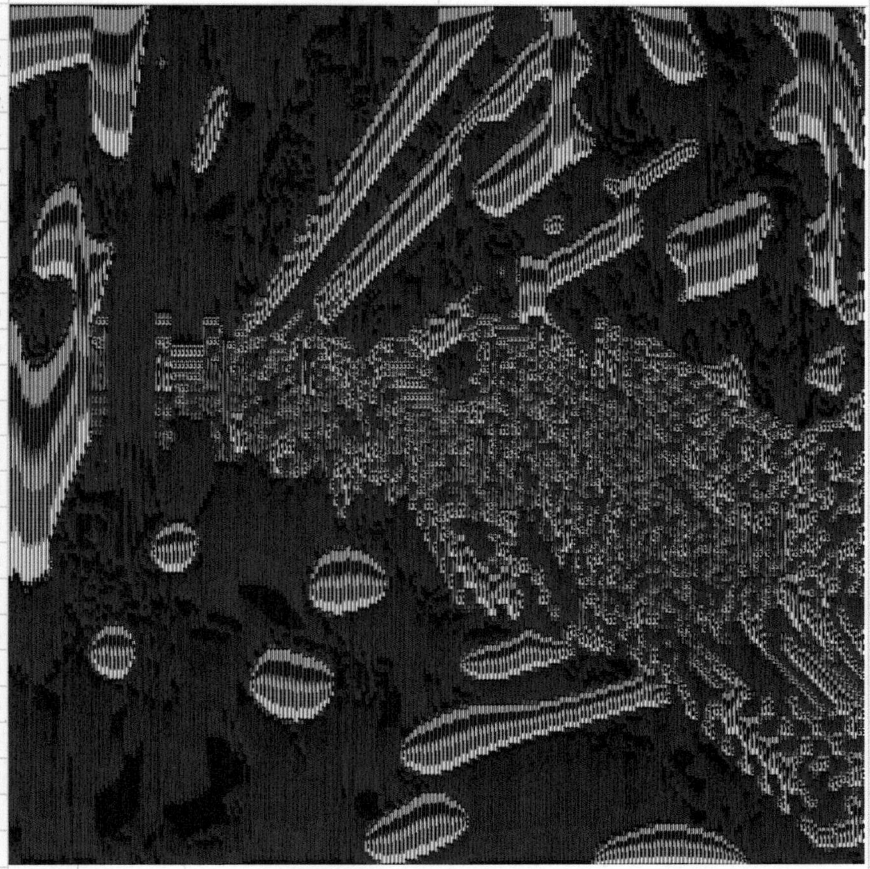

Anti-Environments

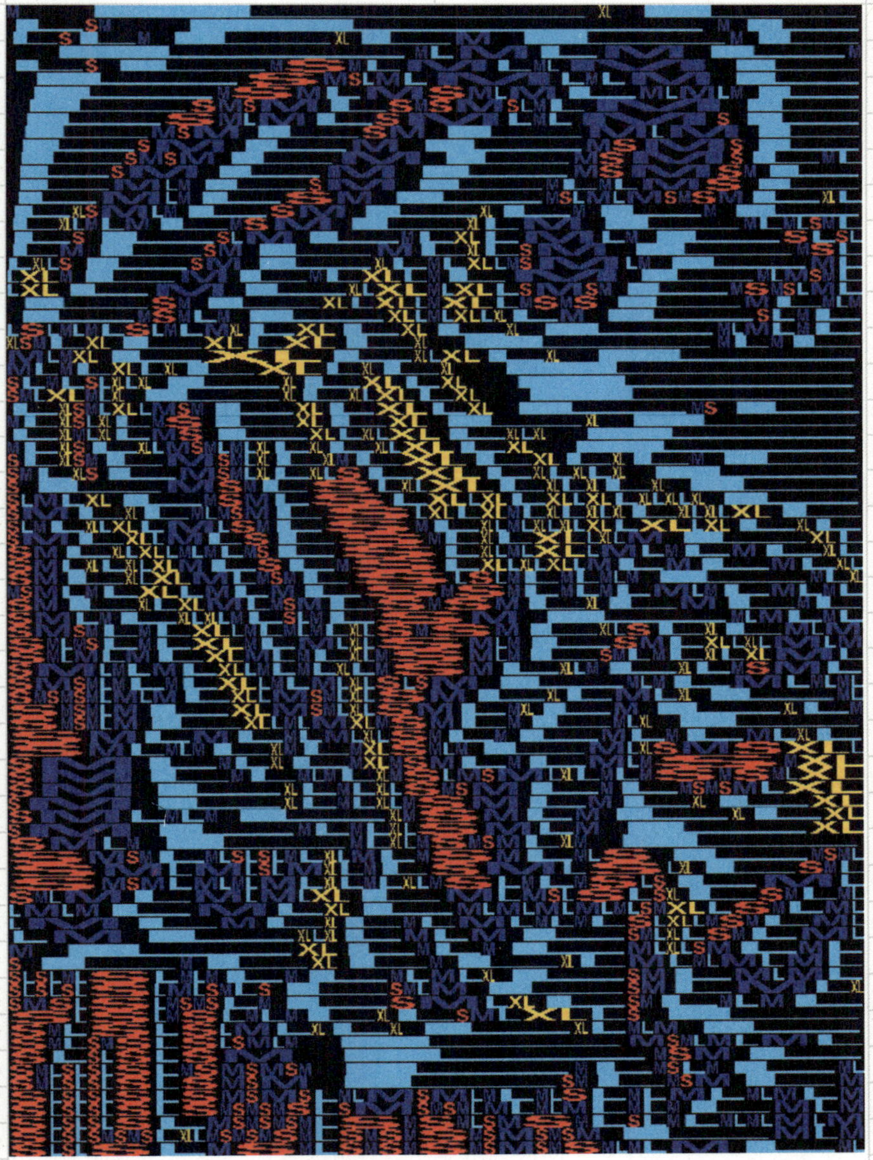

Accordion Tool

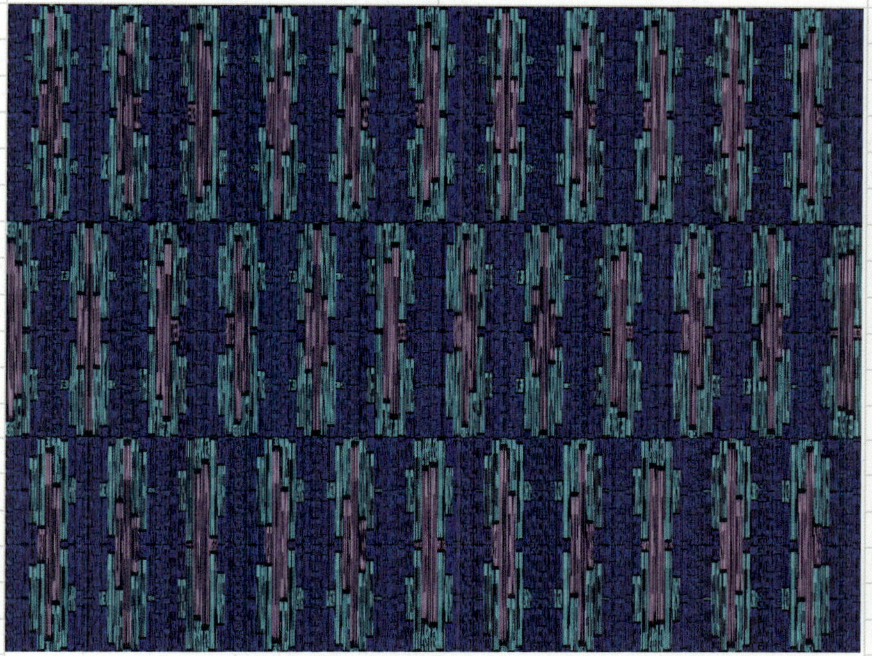

SHAPING TOOLS ARE SHAPING
SHAPING TOOLS ARE SHAPING US SHAPING
US SHAPING TOOLS ARE SHAPING
SHAPING TOOLS ARE SHAPING
SHAPING TOOLS ARE US SHAPING

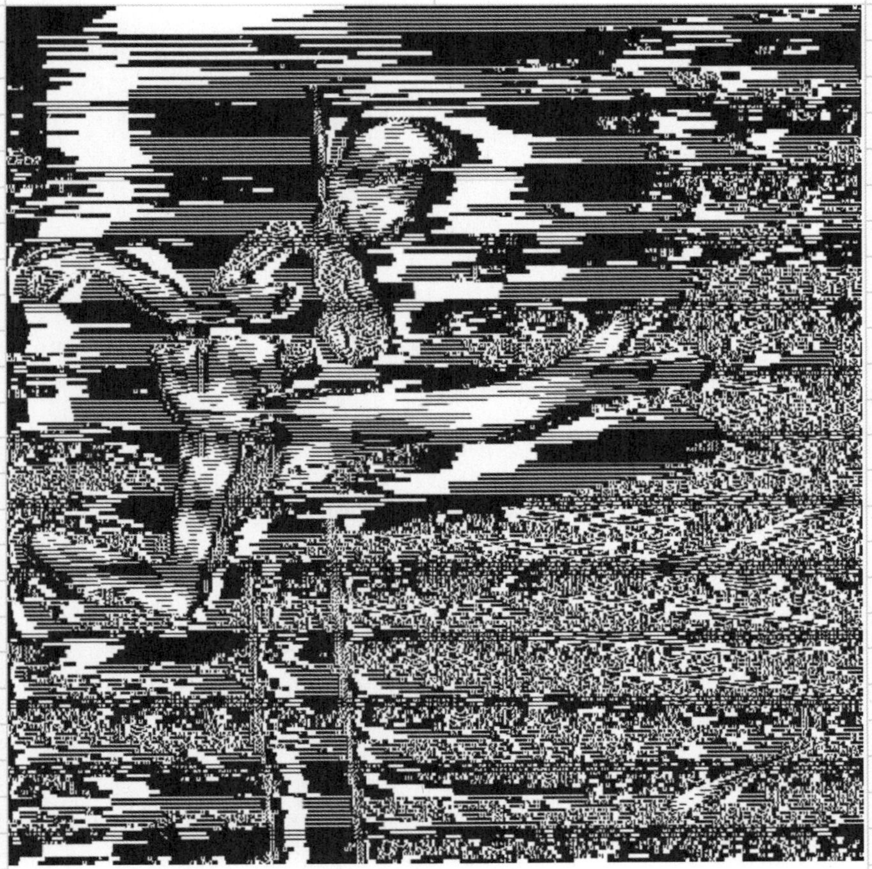

The Open Type Face (OTF) font generator allows anyone to create their own typeface. It addresses the tension between generalization and the growing desire for personalization. To generate customized fonts, it collects user data, including personal characteristics such as facial features, height, weight, gender, or age.

The parameters are mainly captured using the camera. This enables users to influence the design process by, for example, tilting their head, opening their mouth, or pulling a face in front of the computer. In addition, situational information is incorporated into the dataset, which serves as the basis for generating a typeface that reflects a personalized, data-driven design.

Open Type Face

Open Type Face (OTF) links aesthetic possibilities directly to personal parameters. In doing so, it departs from anonymous forms and opens pathways for individual expression. Typeface attributes are tied to factors such as perceived age, proportions, or facial expressions, all captured through the camera. As a result, certain settings remain inaccessible or require the involvement of a second person. Design thus emerges in relation to bodily and social conditions. The unfamiliar mode of interaction shifts the process. What is produced is not only a typeface, but also an expanded human–object relationship. While most software today is controlled via keyboards, touchpads, or screens, keeping the body largely static, OTF actively engages larger parts of the body. Here, movement is not minimized but turned into the driving force of design.

This physical dimension extends beyond the design process itself. Using OTF generates resonance in the analogue space during digital production, sparking curiosity and attention among those present. Digital design becomes more than a result on the screen. It is also a happening in the social sphere, a process that weaves together aesthetic, physical, and communicative dimensions.

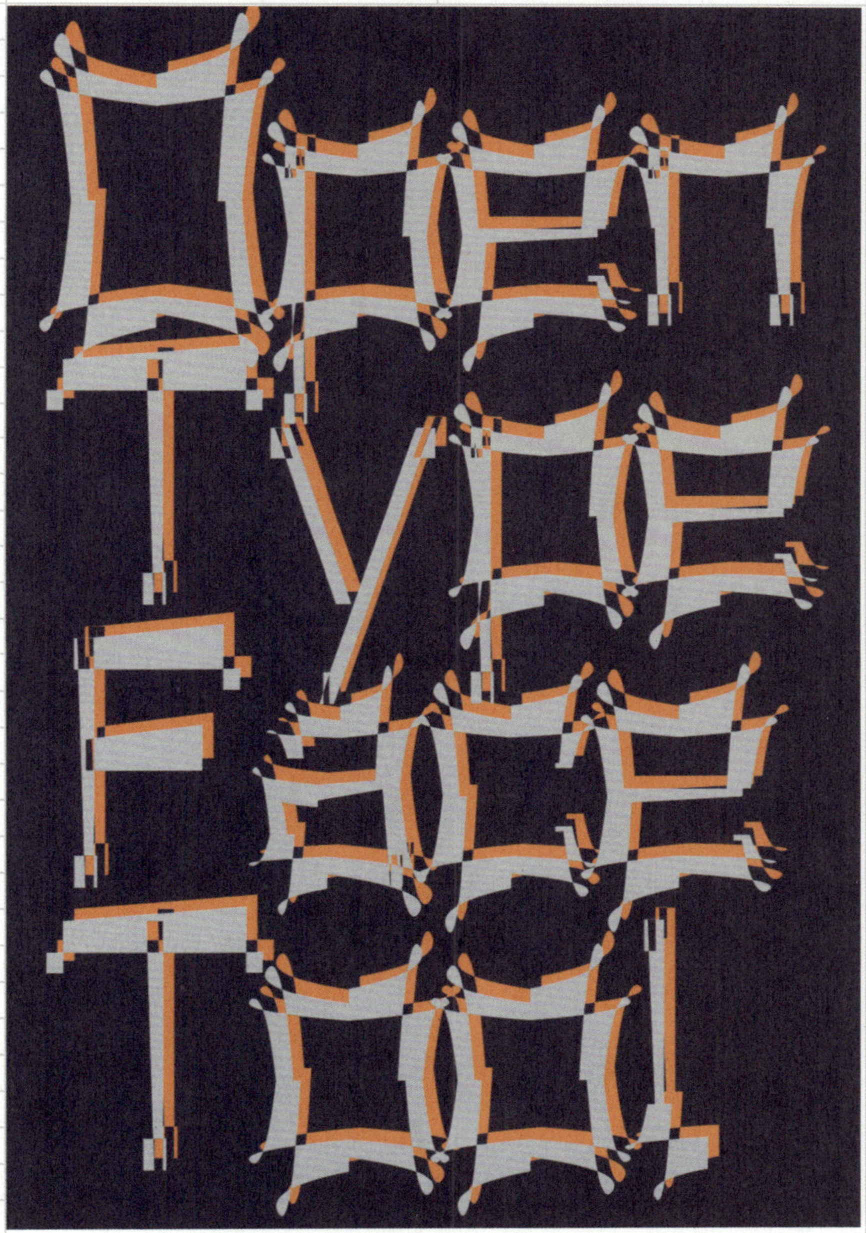

TO FACILITATE THE HUMAN DESIRE FOR EXPLORATION, **WE NEED** TO DESIGN **SITUATED DISTORTIONS** THAT TRIGGER **CURIOSITY.**

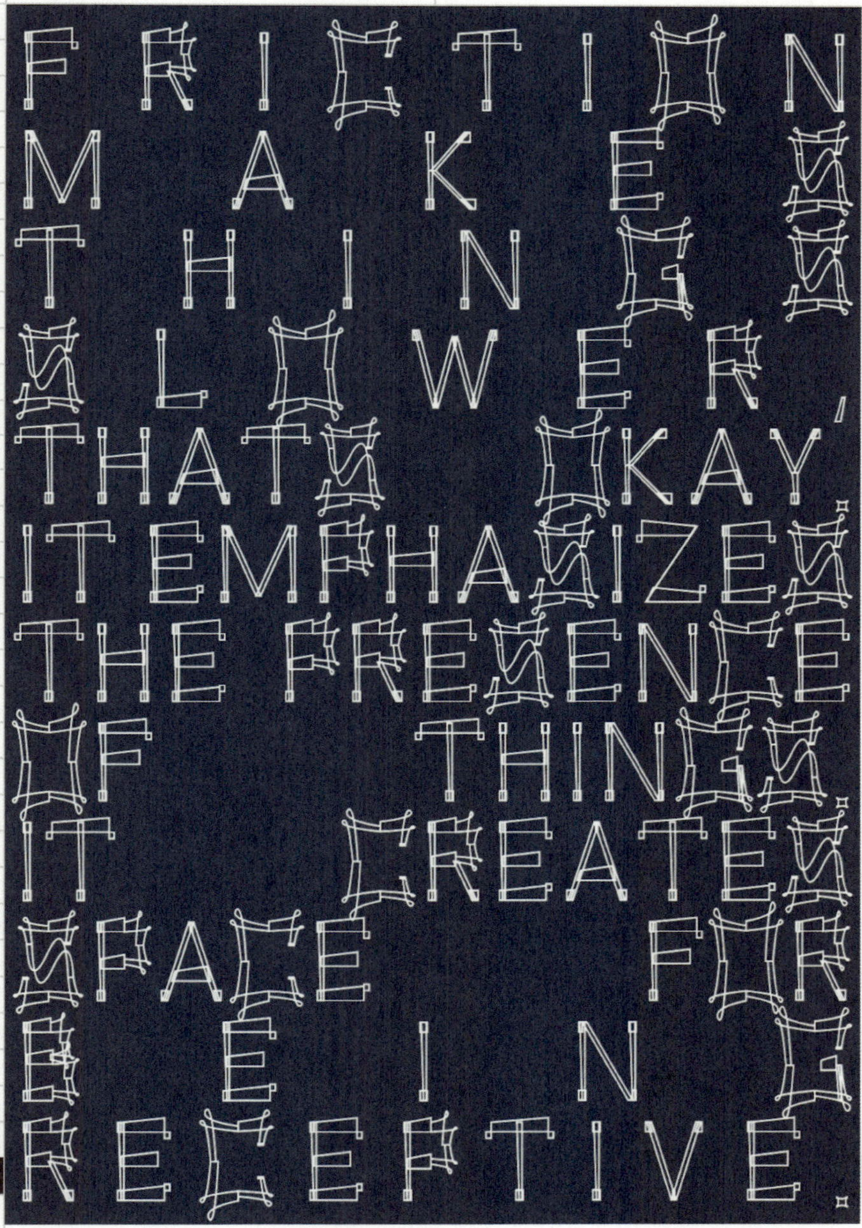
FRICTION
MAKES
THINGS
SLOWER,
THAT'S OKAY
IT EMPHASIZES
THE PRESENCE
OF THINGS,
IT CREATES
SPACE FOR
BEING
RECEPTIVE.

TextEdit

This simple text editor comes pre-installed on Apple devices and provides basic word-processing functions. The user interface is kept minimalistic. It consists of a plain window with a toolbar with options for text formatting, fonts, and paragraph styling. TextEdit supports both plain text and formatted (rich text) files. It also allows you to insert images, links, and tables, and to open and edit file formats such as RTF, DOC, and HTML. As it is so easy to use, TextEdit is well suited for quick notes, minor text edits, and creating simple documents.

TextEdit was introduced in 2001 with the first version of Mac OS X as the default replacement for the earlier text editor, SimpleText. It has since remained a standard utility included with every Mac OS release.

Text Edit
Text Edit
Text Edit
Text Edit
Text Edit
Text Edit

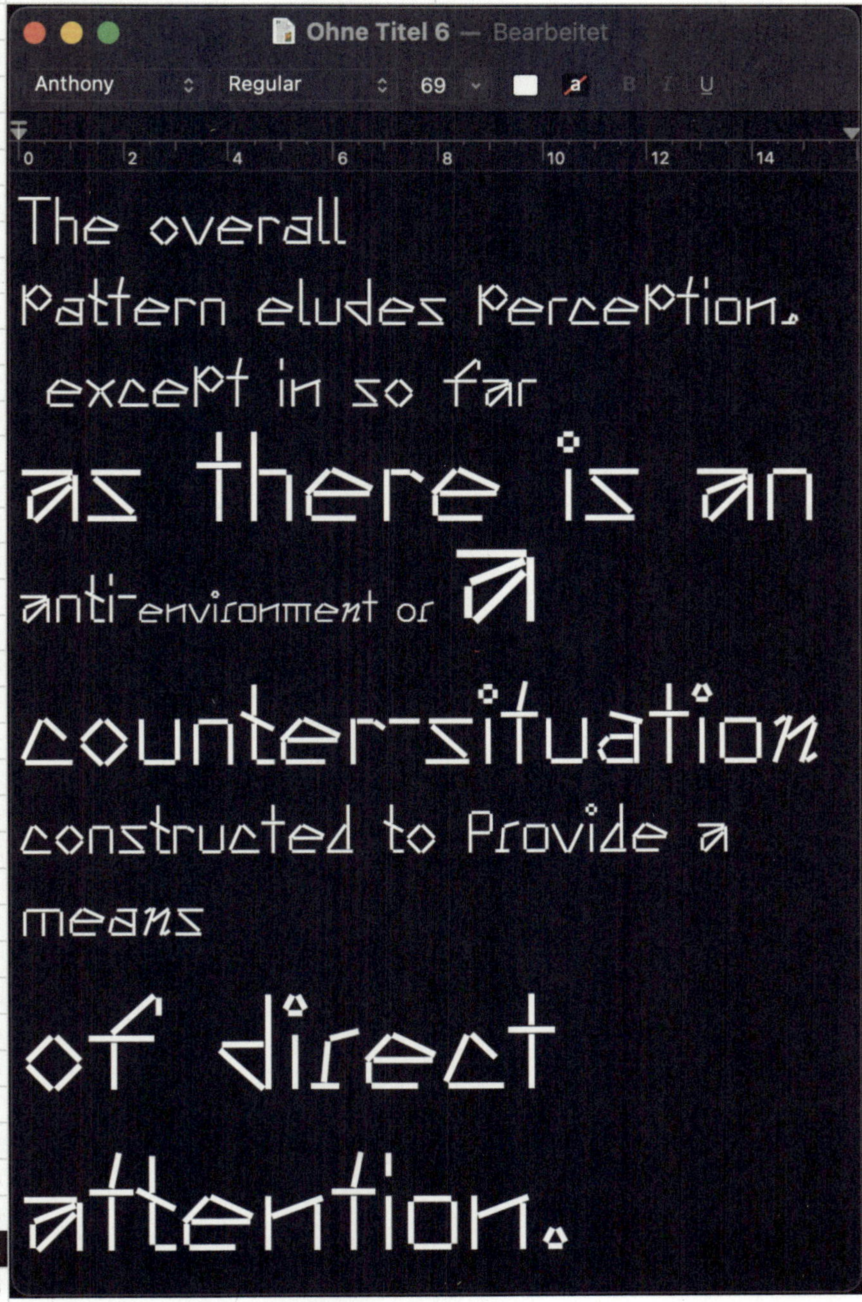
Ohne Titel 6 — Bearbeitet
Anthony
Regular
69
The overall
pattern eludes perception,
except in so far
as there is an
anti-environment or a
counter-situation
constructed to provide a
means
of direct
attention.

Im gonna stay here
untill i feel compfy
I am
gonna
stay here
untill
Im gonna stay here
untill i feel compfy
i feel compfy

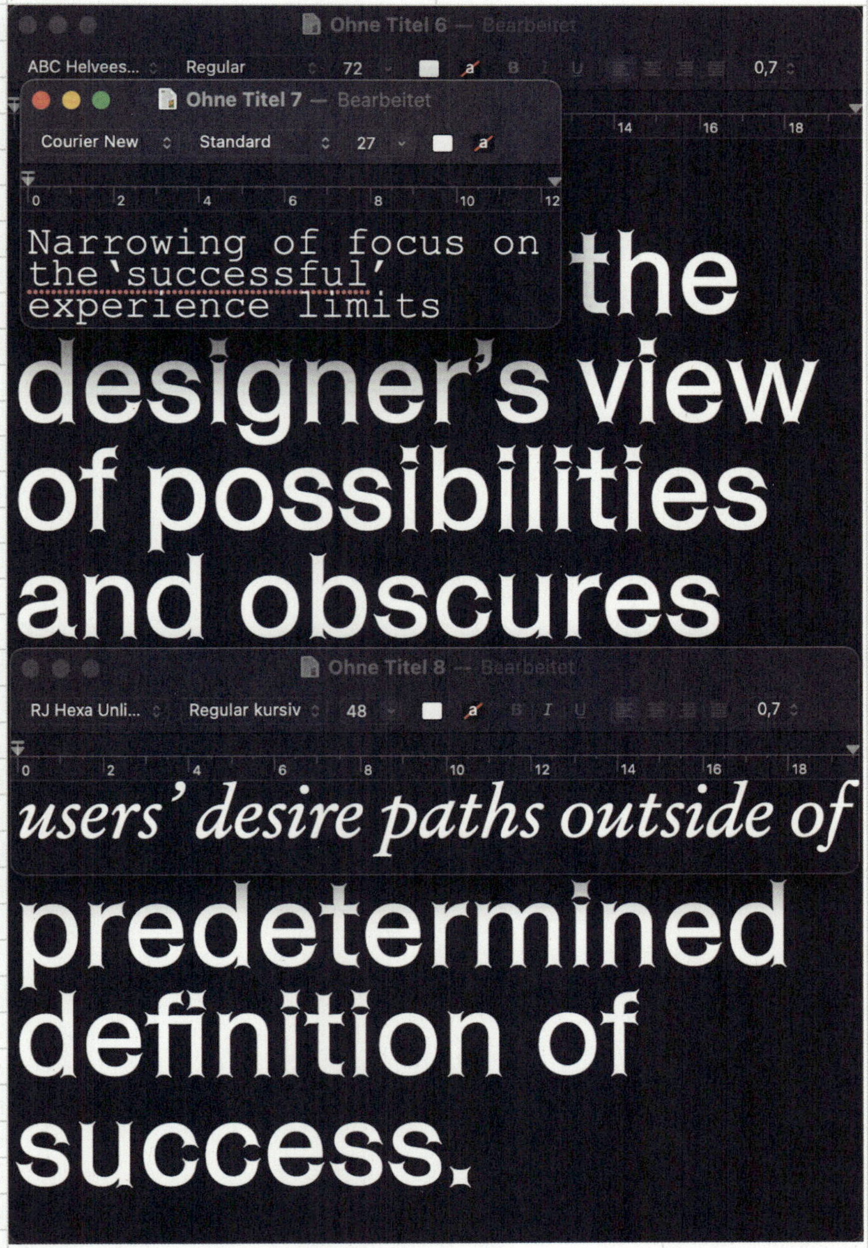
Ohne Titel 6 — Bearbeitet
ABC Helvees...
Regular
72
Ohne Titel 7 — Bearbeitet
Courier New
Standard
27
Narrowing of focus on the 'successful' experience limits
the designer's view of possibilities and obscures
Ohne Titel 8 — Bearbeitet
RJ Hexa Unli...
Regular kursiv
48
users' desire paths outside of
predetermined definition of success.

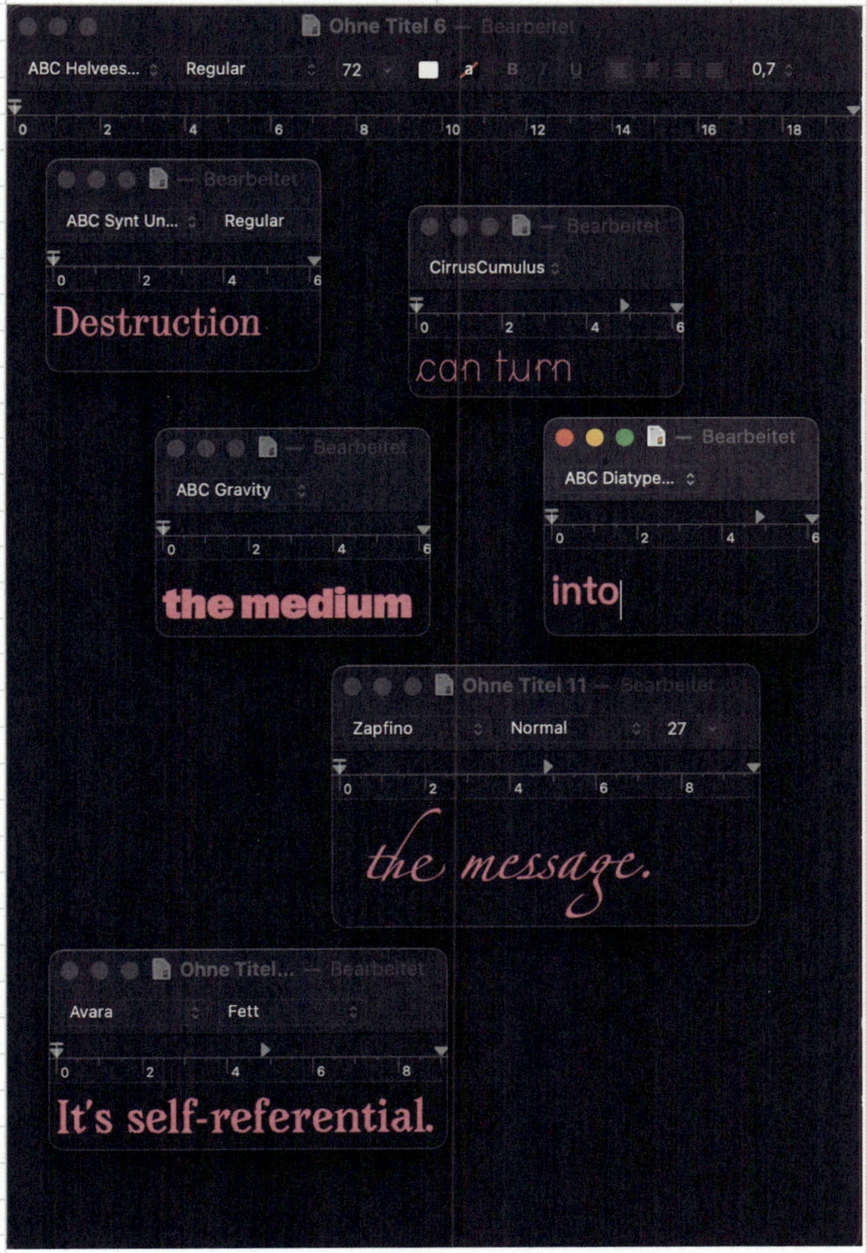
Ohne Titel 6 — Bearbeitet
ABC Helvees...
Regular
72
0,7
Bearbeitet
ABC Synt Un...
Regular
Destruction
Bearbeitet
CirrusCumulus
can turn
Bearbeitet
ABC Gravity
the medium
Bearbeitet
ABC Diatype...
into
Ohne Titel 11 — Bearbeitet
Zapfino
Normal
27
the message.
Ohne Titel... — Bearbeitet
Avara
Fett
It's self-referential.

Adapt
To
the workflow
OR GET
Lost

Chroma Shift Tool

This image-processing tool was developed by Luis Adrian Borchardt as an experiment in exploring color layers. An uploaded image is split into different color layers that can be individually shifted, rotated, or adjusted in transparency. A sidebar provides controls for offsetting, rotating, and adjusting the opacity of each layer, with options to randomize or reset their arrangement.
The central canvas displays the current result in real time, while a small preview box shows each layer separately. The tool aims to provide an alternative approach to image and color manipulation, making it more accessible through targeted adjustment of individual layers.

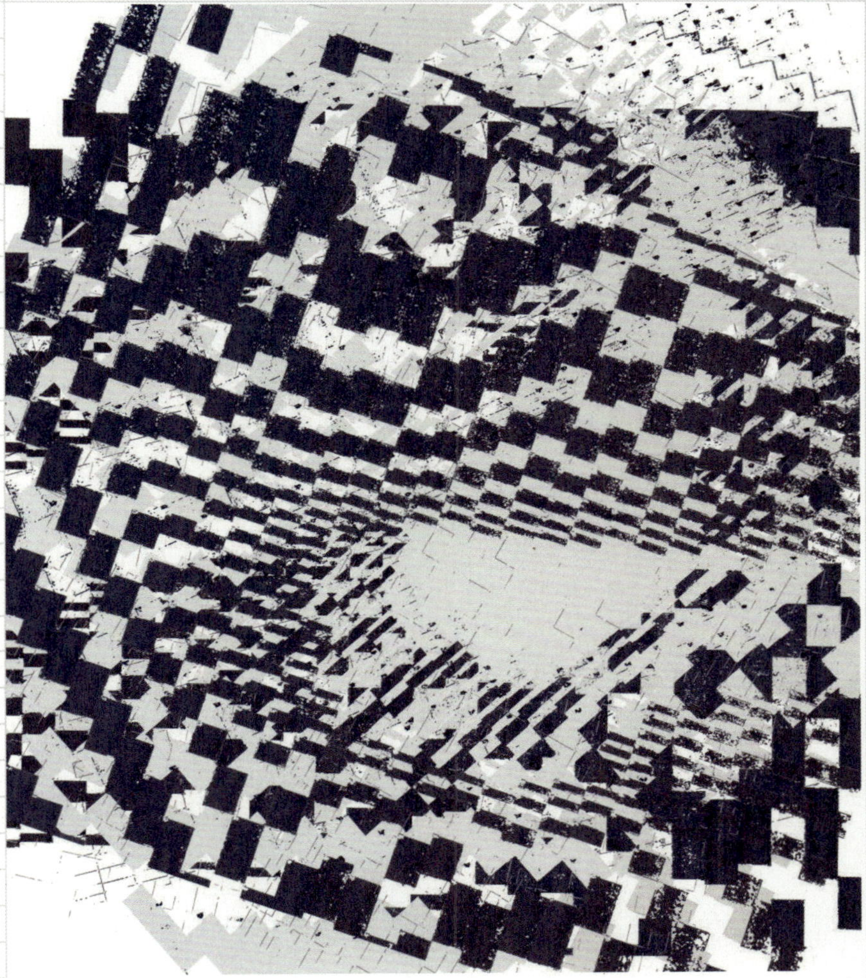

Page 204 | Anti-Environments

Page 205 | Chroma Shift Tool

Brush Sculpt Tool

Brush Sculpt by Luis Adrian Borchardt is a tool for creating entirely individual brushes to be used in drawing. Instead of being limited to predefined shapes, users can either upload their own image or save the current drawing as a new "brush". This permits a creative and personal painting experience, giving users complete freedom in determining the brush's appearance and testing it directly on the canvas.

The tool's strength is that, over time, users can build up their own toolbar of unique shapes, which can continuously be combined to create new, reusable designs. Being drawn by hand rather than generated using geometric presets, the shapes have a more personal and expressive character.

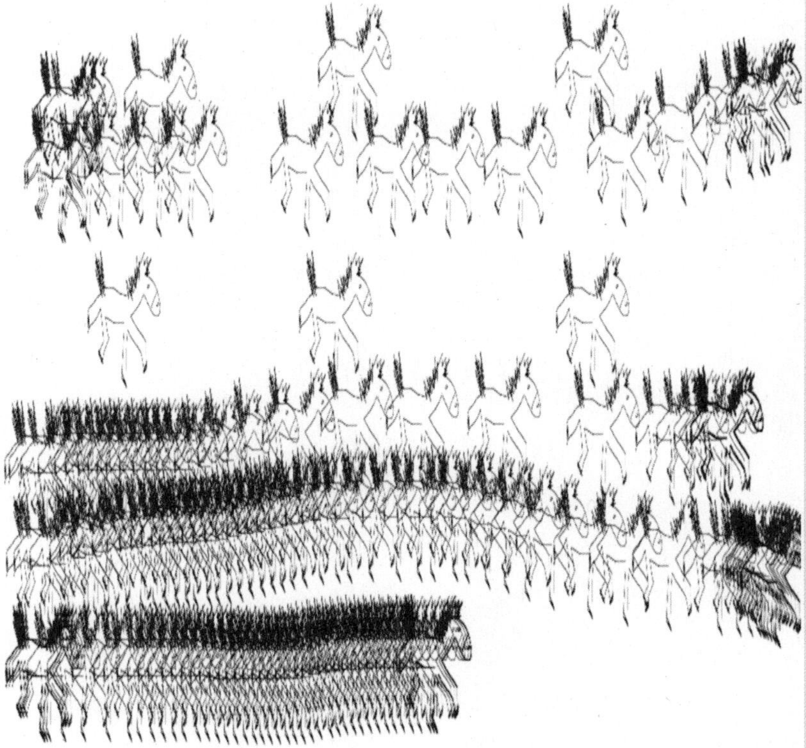

GT Generator

Glitch Type Generator is a browser-based tool developed by Jake Welch that generates glitch effects on text layers. It copies segments of a text content layer and creates random “runners” to produce a glitch-like aesthetic. The tool enables users to create dynamic and randomized distortions for experimental typographic or graphic results. Via the interface, they can input text, adjust color, set the size of the copied sections, and define the starting position of the type. The tool also supports the uploading of custom fonts.

Boundaries
are where
we have to
become
creative.

Embrace
uncomfortable
situations.

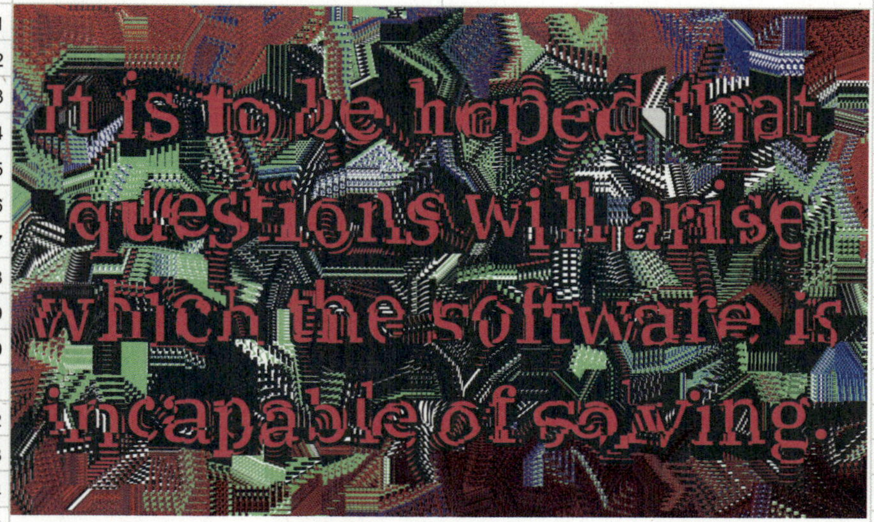
It is to be hoped that
questions will arise
which the software is
incapable of solving.

Friction
leads to
reflection.

Reference Index

01 "Our tools are now often so flawlessly smooth that we stop noticing—let alone questioning—them." Borchardt, L. (2025)

02 "Digital technology has long pursued the goal of eliminating friction." Maurer, L. & Wouters, R. (2023)

03 "We have strived to design 'seamless' digital systems in which users go about completing their goals with little awareness of the underlying technology, where things happen 'automagically'." Lloyd, A., Mancuso, D., Sonis, D. & Hubert, L. (2020)

04 "Tools are convenient, but convenience can also limit exploration and creativity." Borchardt, L. (2025)

05 "All our actions are recorded and translated into data […] This is why my autonomy is at stake." Maurer, L., quoted in Petković, V. (2023)

06 "[…] So, if we are predictable, if our environment is predictable, a few people can control it better." Petković, V. (2023)

07 "As designers we have been relentless about prioritizing ease-of-use, identifying friction and eradicating it from the interactions we design." Lloyd, A., Mancuso, D., Sonis, D. & Hubert, L. (2020)

08 "[…] it is exactly in friction that things become clearer to him and the danger of them escaping him is what makes them more desirable." Fellini, F., quoted in Petković, V. (2023)

09 Friction initiates movement; without movement, there remains a state of stagnation. cf. Maurer, L. (2024)

10 "If you have a ball, you throw it; if you have a chair, you sit on it. But digital devices are characterized by the fact that regardless of the function, you treat them the same way […] Interaction gets trimmed down to your fingertips." Sheikh, H., quoted in Maurer, L. (2023)

11 "[…] pervasive computing is the norm." Souza, A., Loureiro, A. A. F. & Oliveira, L. B. (2019)

12 "Software is a commercial mass product, so it is not made for individuals but for a target group with hypothetical wishes and demands." Middendorp, J. (2000)

13 "Adapt to workflows, or get lost." Borchardt, L. (2025)

14 "Now there is a danger that designers will only function properly if their creativity does not exceed the potential of their computer: if the world of ideas fits inside the world of tools." Middendorp, J. (2000)

15 If all you have is a hammer, everything looks like a nail. cf. Maslow, A. H. (1966)

16 "Instant gratification is what digital technology currently optimizes for. This results in the loss of desire, waiting and boredom." Maurer, L. & Wouters, R. (2023)

17 "Being bored lets you start new fascinations. Boredom gets us into productive flow. When friction acts to slow things down it allows us to step into the now." Maurer, L. & Wouters, R. (2023)

18 Human messiness counteracts the goal of prediction. cf. Maurer, L. & Wouters, R. (2023)

19 "Create situations that are not predicted, measured and calculated beforehand; situations that result from and amount to the present moment." Maurer, L. & Wouters, R. (2023)

20 "I've become too passive with my tools. I don't invent, I don't yearn. I manage, I cope." Borchardt, L. (2025)

21 "Manipulating tools leads you to a more personal creative process. Instead of adapting to a given one." Borchardt, L. (2025)

22 “Unforeseen actions are all frictions.”
Maurer, L. & Wouters, R. (2023)

23 Creating friction means starting to have meaningful interactions with tools. cf. Maurer, L. (2024)

24 “De-automize.” Borchardt, L. (2025)

25 “If it works, it’s obsolete.” McLuhan, M. (2010)

26 “Perhaps our attention wanders if there are no rough edges.”
Middendorp, J. (2000)

27 “Disrupt the prevailing narrative of convenience at any cost.”
Maurer, L. & Wouters, R. (2023)

28 “Every shortcut you internalize creates a larger distance between you and something new.” Borchardt, L. (2025)

29 “When interacting with screens we lack resistance. Swiping screens makes our world more superficial. Human life gains depth when having thing-relations.” Maurer, L. & Wouters, R. (2023)

30 Engage with your whole body.
cf. Maurer, L. (2024)

31 “To facilitate the human desire for exploration, we need to design situated distortions that trigger curiosity.” Hobye, M. (2014)

32 Curiosity can be evoked through novelty, partial exposure, complexity, uncertainty and conflict.
cf. Tieben, R., Bekker, T. & Schouten, B. (2011)

33 “Friction makes things slower, that’s okay. It emphasizes the presence of things. It creates space for being receptive.” cf. Maurer, L. & Wouters, R. (2023)

34 “Search for the complicated, the new, modify, build, break, request.” Borchardt, L. (2025)

35 “The overall pattern eludes perception except in so far as there is an anti-environment or a counter-situation constructed to provide a means of direct attention.”
McLuhan, M., & Moos, M. A. (1997)

36 “Narrowing of focus on the ‘successful’ experience limits the designer’s view of possibilities and obscures users’ desired paths outside of predetermined definition of success.”
Lloyd, A., Mancuso, D., Sonis, D. & Hubert, L. (2020)

37 “Destruction turns the medium into the message. It’s self-referential.” Lauritzsen, S. (2022)

38 Feel structures you are not adjusted to; you can learn and discover. cf. Maurer, L. & Wouters, R. (2023)

39 “Boundaries are where we have to become creative.”
Borchardt, L. (2025)

40 “Embrace uncomfortable situations.” Maurer, L. & Wouters, R. (2023)

41 “It is to be hoped that questions will arise which the software is incapable of solving.” Middendorp, J. (2000)

42 “Friction leads to reflection.”
Borchardt, L. (2025)

1. Borchardt, L. (2025).

2. Maurer, L. & Wouters, R. (2023):
Designing Friction.
Available at: https://designingfriction.com/
(last viewed: 24.9.2025).

3. Lloyd, A., Mancuso, D., Sonis, D. & Hubert, L. (2020):
Camera Obscura: Beyond the lens of user-centered design. Medium.
Available at: https://alexis.medium.com/camera-obscura-beyond-the-lens-of-user-centered-design-631bb4f37594
(last viewed: 24.9.2025).

4. Borchardt, L. (2025).

5. Maurer, L., quoted in Petković, V. (2023):
IDFA DocLab opens: Designing Phenomenal Friction. IDFA – International Documentary Film Festival Amsterdam.
Available at: https://professionals.idfa.nl/stories/idfa-doclab-opens-designing-phenomenal-friction/
(last viewed: 24.9.2025).

6. Petković, V. (2023):
IDFA DocLab opens: Designing Phenomenal Friction. IDFA – International Documentary Film Festival Amsterdam.
Available at: https://professionals.idfa.nl/stories/idfa-doclab-opens-designing-phenomenal-friction/
(last viewed: 24.9.2025).

7. Lloyd, A., Mancuso, D., Sonis, D. & Hubert, L. (2020):
Camera Obscura: Beyond the lens of user-centered design. Medium.
Available at: https://alexis.medium.com/camera-obscura-beyond-the-lens-of-user-centered-design-631bb4f37594
(last viewed: 24.9.2025).

8. Fellini, F., quoted in Petković, V. (2023):
IDFA DocLab opens Designing Phenomenal Friction. IDFA – International Documentary Film Festival Amsterdam.
Available at: https://professionals.idfa.nl/stories/idfa-doclab-opens-designing-phenomenal-friction/
(last viewed: 24.9.2025).

9. cf. Maurer, L. (2024):
Talk at Iterations 2024.
Available at: https://www.youtube.com/live/VhqmF4PNIfc
(last viewed: 24.9.2025).

10. Sheikh, H., quoted in Maurer, L., in Petković, V. (2023):
IDFA DocLab opens Designing Phenomenal Friction. IDFA – International Documentary Film Festival Amsterdam.
Available at: https://professionals.idfa.nl/stories/idfa-doclab-opens-designing-phenomenal-friction/
(last viewed: 24.9.2025).

11. Souza, A., Loureiro, A. A. F. & Oliveira, L. B. (2019):
Challenges and Directions for
Authentication in Pervasive Computing.
Available at: https://arxiv.org/abs/1907.05214
(last viewed: 24.9.2025).

12. Middendorp, J. (2000):
Toolspace. LettError.
Available at: https://letterror.com/articles/toolspace.html
(last viewed: 24.9.2025).

13. Borchardt, L. (2025).

14. Middendorp, J. (2000):
Toolspace. LettError.
Available at: https://letterror.com/articles/toolspace.html
(last viewed: 24.9.2025).

15. cf. Maslow, A.H. (1966):
The Psychology of Science: A Reconnaissance.
Anna Maria, FL: Maurice Bassett Publishing, p.15.

16. Maurer, L. & Wouters, R. (2023):
Designing Friction.
Available at: https://designingfriction.com/
(last viewed: 24.9.2025).

17. Maurer, L. & Wouters, R. (2023):
Designing Friction.
Available at: https://designingfriction.com/
(last viewed: 24.9.2025).

18. cf. Maurer, L. & Wouters, R. (2023):
Designing Friction.
Available at: https://designingfriction.com/
(last viewed: 24.9.2025).

19. Maurer, L. & Wouters, R. (2023):
Designing Friction.
Available at: https://designingfriction.com/
(last viewed: 24.9.2025).

20. Borchardt, L. (2025).

21. Borchardt, L. (2025).

22. Maurer, L. & Wouters, R. (2023):
Designing Friction.
Available at: https://designingfriction.com/
(last viewed: 24.9.2025).

23. cf. Maurer, L. (2024):
Talk at Iterations 2024.
Available at: https://www.youtube.com/live/VhqmF4PNIfc
(last viewed: 24.9.2025).

24. Borchardt, L. (2025).

25. McLuhan, M. (2010):
The Medium and the Light:
Reflections on Religion and Media. Eugene,
OR: Wipf and Stock Publishers, p.139.

26. Middendorp, J. (2000):
Toolspace. LettError.
Available at: https://letterror.com/articles/toolspace.html
(last viewed: 24.9.2025).

27. Maurer, L. & Wouters, R. (2023):
Embracing Friction:
A conversation with Luna Maurer and Roel Wouters.
Branch – A Sustainable Internet for All.
Available at: https://branch.climateaction.tech/issues/author/luna-maurer/
(last viewed: 24.9.2025).

28. Borchardt, L. (2025).

29. Maurer, L. & Wouters, R. (2023):
Designing Friction.
Available at: https://designingfriction.com/
(last viewed: 24.9.2025).

30. cf. Maurer, L. (2024):
Talk at Iterations 2024.
Available at: https://www.youtube.com/live/VhqmF4PNIfc
(last viewed: 24.9.2025).

31. Hobye, M. (2014):
Designing for Homo Explorens:
Open Social Play in Performative Frames.
Doktorarbeit, Malmö University,
School of Arts and Communication – K3.
Available at: http://dspace.mah.se/handle/2043/16510
(last viewed: 24.9.2025).

32. Hobye, M. (2014):
Designing for Homo Explorens:
Open Social Play in Performative Frames.
Doktorarbeit, Malmö University,
School of Arts and Communication – K3.
Available at: http://dspace.mah.se/handle/2043/16510
(last viewed: 24.9.2025).

33. cf. Tieben, R., Bekker, T. and Schouten, B. (2011):
Curiosity and Interaction: Making People Curious through Interactive Systems.
Proceedings of the 8th International Conference on Advances in Computer Entertainment Technology (ACE 2011), Lisbon, Portugal, pp. 362–363.

33. cf. Maurer, L. & Wouters, R. (2023):
Designing Friction.
Available at: https://designingfriction.com/
(last viewed: 24.9.2025).

34. Borchardt, L. (2025).

35. McLuhan, M., & Moos, M. A. (1997):
The relation of environment to anti-environment.
In Media Research (p. 11).
London: Routledge.
Available at: https://doi.org/10.4324/9781315078601-9
(last viewed: 24.9.2025).

36. Lloyd, A., Mancuso, D., Sonis, D. & Hubert, L. (2020):
Camera Obscura: Beyond the Lens of User-Centered Design. Medium.
Available at: https://alexis.medium.com/camera-obscura-beyond-the-lens-of-user-centered-design-631bb4f37594
(last viewed: 24.9.2025).

37. Lauritzsen, S. (2022):
Five Types of Design Friction and Why They’re Awesome. Medium
Available at: https://medium.com/@syverlauritz/five-types-of-design-friction-and-why-theyre-awesome-11f850072b8f
(last viewed: 24.9.2025).

38. cf. Maurer, L. & Wouters, R. (2023):
Designing Friction.
Available at: https://designingfriction.com/
(last viewed: 24.9.2025).

39. Borchardt, L. (2025).

40. Maurer, L. & Wouters, R. (2023):
Designing Friction.
Available at: https://designingfriction.com/
(last viewed: 24.9.2025).

41. Middendorp, J. (2000):
Toolspace. LettError.
Available at: https://letterror.com/articles/toolspace.html
(last viewed: 24.9.2025).

42. Borchardt, L. (2025).

Using Apps Script and the DriveApp API, images are retrieved from a Google-Drive folder, sorted in a set order, and generated as URLs. The script then places these images automatically into predefined areas of the spreadsheet and scales them to the maximum width. It also creates new sheets, adds page numbers, and inserts the images according to a predefined sequence. Overall, the layout is generated dynamically from the image file names, while still following a fixed structure.

```
function insertImagesAndNumberPages() {
  try {
    var props =
PropertiesService.getScriptProperties();
    var imageIndex =
parseInt(props.getProperty("imageIndex") || "0", 10);
    var pageNumber =
parseInt(props.getProperty("pageNumber") || "16",
10);
    var previousGroup =
props.getProperty("previousGroup") || null;

    var folderId =
"1MzbLNJIEUB_SRdAQ62euwEp4-foMAvGe";
    var folder = DriveApp.getFolderById(folderId);
    var files = folder.getFiles();

    var imageUrls = [];
    while (files.hasNext()) {
      var file = files.next();
      if (file.getMimeType().startsWith("image/")) {
        var fileId = file.getId();
        var fileUrl = "https://drive.google.com/uc?id=" +
fileId;
        var fileName = file.getName();
```



```
        var match =
fileName.match(/^([A-Za-z]{2})(\d+(?:\.\d+)?)/);
        if (match) {
          var group = match[1];
          var number = parseFloat(match[2]);
          imageUrls.push({ group: group, number:
number, url: fileUrl });
        }
      }
    }
    imageUrls.sort(function (a, b) {
      return a.group === b.group ? a.number -
b.number : a.group.localeCompare(b.group);
    });

    var ss =
SpreadsheetApp.getActiveSpreadsheet();
    var deckblattTemplate =
ss.getSheetByName("Deckblatt");
    if (!deckblattTemplate) {
      throw new Error("Das Tabellenblatt 'Deckblatt'
als Vorlage wurde nicht gefunden.");
    }

    var specialCases = {
      "BP-CA": 2,
      "IM-JG": 3,
      "AM-BP": 1,
      "PD-QO": 2,
      "EK-FS": 2
    };

    var maxIterations = 10;
    var iterations = 0;

    while (imageIndex < imageUrls.length &&
iterations < maxIterations) {
      var currentImage = imageUrls[imageIndex];
      var currentGroup = currentImage.group;

      if (previousGroup && currentGroup !==
previousGroup) {
        var specialKey =
`${previousGroup}-${currentGroup}`;
        var blankPages = specialCases[specialKey] ||
1;

        for (var i = 0; i < blankPages; i++) {
          var blankSheet =
deckblattTemplate.copyTo(ss);
          blankSheet.setName(`Blank_${pageNumber
/ 2}`);
          formatPageNumbering(blankSheet,
pageNumber, true, "B", "J", "D", "L");
          pageNumber++;
          formatPageNumbering(blankSheet,
pageNumber, false, "B", "J", "D", "L");
          pageNumber++;

          // Bilder nur bei Standardwechsel einfügen
(nicht bei Sonderfällen)
          if (!specialCases[specialKey] && i === 0 &&
imageIndex < imageUrls.length) {
            insertSingleImage(blankSheet,
imageUrls[imageIndex].url, "J2:O2");
            imageIndex++;
          }
        }
      }

      previousGroup = currentGroup;

      var newSheet = deckblattTemplate.copyTo(ss);
      newSheet.setName(`Seite_${pageNumber /
2}`);
      processSheet(newSheet, imageIndex,
imageUrls);
      formatPageNumbering(newSheet,
pageNumber, true, "B", "J", "D", "L");
      pageNumber++;
      formatPageNumbering(newSheet,
pageNumber, false, "B", "J", "D", "L");
      pageNumber++;

      imageIndex += 2;
      iterations++;
    }

    props.setProperties({
```



```
      imageIndex: imageIndex,
      pageNumber: pageNumber,
      previousGroup: previousGroup
    });

    if (imageIndex < imageUrls.length) {

ScriptApp.newTrigger("insertImagesAndNumberPa
ges")
        .timeBased()
        .after(1000)
        .create();
    } else {
      SpreadsheetApp.getUi().alert("Verarbeitung
abgeschlossen!");
      props.deleteAllProperties();
    }
  } catch (error) {
    Logger.log("Fehler: " + error.message);
  }
}

function formatPageNumbering(sheet,
pageNumber, isLeft = true, colStartLeft = "B",
colStartRight = "J", colEndLeft = "D", colEndRight =
"L") {
  var colStart = isLeft ? colStartLeft : colStartRight;
  var colEnd = isLeft ? colEndLeft : colEndRight;

sheet.getRange(`${colStart}42:${colEnd}43`).setVal
ue(`Seite ${pageNumber.toString().padStart(2,
"0")}`);

sheet.getRange(`${colStart}42:${colEnd}43`).setFo
ntSize(12);
}

function scaleImageToFitRange(image, range,
sheet) {
  var totalWidth = 0;
  var columns = range.getNumColumns();
  for (var col = 0; col < columns; col++) {
    totalWidth +=
sheet.getColumnWidth(range.getColumn() + col);
  }

  var originalWidth = image.getWidth();
  var originalHeight = image.getHeight();
  var scaleFactor = totalWidth / originalWidth;
  var newHeight = originalHeight * scaleFactor;

  image.setWidth(totalWidth);
  image.setHeight(newHeight);
}

function processSheet(sheet, imageIndex,
imageUrls) {
  if (imageIndex < imageUrls.length) {
    var firstImageUrl = imageUrls[imageIndex].url;
    var firstImageRange = sheet.getRange("B2:G2");
    var firstCell = sheet.getRange("B2");
    var firstImage = sheet.insertImage(firstImageUrl,
firstCell.getColumn(), firstCell.getRow());
    scaleImageToFitRange(firstImage,
```

```
firstImageRange, sheet);
  }

  if (imageIndex + 1 < imageUrls.length) {
    var secondImageUrl = imageUrls[imageIndex +
1].url;
    var secondImageRange =
sheet.getRange("J2:O2");
    var secondCell = sheet.getRange("J2");
    var secondImage =
sheet.insertImage(secondImageUrl,
secondCell.getColumn(), secondCell.getRow());
    scaleImageToFitRange(secondImage,
secondImageRange, sheet);
  }
}

function insertSingleImage(sheet, imageUrl, range)
{
  var targetRange = sheet.getRange(range);
  var cell = targetRange.getCell(1, 1);
  var image = sheet.insertImage(imageUrl,
cell.getColumn(), cell.getRow());
  scaleImageToFitRange(image, targetRange,
sheet);
}
```


Anti-Environments
On the Exploration of Unconventional Tools through Friction and Norm-Bending
by Luis Adrian Borchardt

Bachelor of Arts
2024/25
Hochschule Mainz

Supervisors:
Alexander Roidl,
Katja Davar

Texts, images, design, and concept: Luis Adrian Borchardt

Copy editing and proofreading: Jane Eggers
Font: Arial Regular
Paper: Holmen TRND, 80 g/m2
Printing and binding:
Druckhaus Sportflieger GmbH, Berlin

Distribution in Germany, Hong Kong, Japan, Singapore, South Korea, and Taiwan:
einBuch.haus
Lindenstrasse 91
10969 Berlin
Germany
www.einbuch.haus
E info@einbuch.haus

Distribution in all other countries:
Verlag Scheidegger & Spiess AG
Niederdorfstrasse 54
8001 Zürich
Switzerland
www.scheidegger-spiess.ch
T +41 44 262 16 62
E info@scheidegger-spiess.ch

Product safety
Responsible person pursuant to EU Regulation 2023/988 (GPSR):
GVA Gemeinsame Verlagsauslieferung Göttingen GmbH & Co. KG
Post Box 2021
37010 Göttingen
Germany
T +49 551 384 200 0
E info@gva-verlage.de

Scheidegger & Spiess is being supported by the Federal Office of Culture with a general subsidy for the years 2026–2028.

English edition: ISBN 978-3-03942-337-8
German edition: ISBN 978-3-03942-336-1